MW00466797

Praise for *The Science of the Dogon*

"Not only is the Dogon creation myth resplendent in its sheer beauty, but it reflects the nuances of cutting-edge scientific cosmology better than any other in the world, and finally this is being recognized for the first time. Laird Scranton's *The Science of the Dogon* becomes a quintessential read for anyone wishing to learn the truth about this most fascinating and much-maligned subject."

ANDREW COLLINS,
AUTHOR OF *THE CYGNUS MYSTERY* AND
FROM THE ASHES OF ANGELS

"*The Science of the Dogon* decodes the opaque symbols of Dogon creation myth with great ingenuity backed by solid scholarship. Highly recommended."

IDA P. MOFFETT,
EDITOR AND COPUBLISHER OF *THE PALE FOX*

"*The Science of the Dogon* takes the study of the ancients to an exciting new level. Laird has cracked the visual code of the Dogon, and his explanations are thoroughly supported."

WILLIAM HENRY,
AUTHOR OF *EGYPT: STARGATE DISCOVERIES* VIDEO SERIES AND
GUEST HOST OF "DREAMLAND" WITH WHITLEY STRIEBER

THE SCIENCE
OF THE
DOGON

DECODING THE AFRICAN
MYSTERY TRADITION

LAIRD SCRANTON

Foreword by John Anthony West

Inner Traditions
Rochester, Vermont

Inner Traditions
One Park Street
Rochester, Vermont 05767
www.InnerTraditions.com

Copyright © 2002, 2006 by Laird Scranton

Originally published in 2002 by Xlibris as *Hidden Meanings: A Study of the Founding Symbols of Civilization*

All rights reserved. No part of this book may be reproduced or utilized in any form or by any means, electronic or mechanical, including photocopying, recording, or by any information storage and retrieval system, without permission in writing from the publisher.

Library of Congress Cataloging-in-Publication Data
Scranton, Laird, 1953–
  [Hidden meanings]
  The science of the Dogon : decoding the African mystery tradition / Laird Scranton.
    p. cm.
  "Originally published in 2002 by Xlibris as Hidden meanings : a study of the founding symbols of civilization"—T.p. verso.
  Includes bibliographical references and index.
  ISBN-13: 978-1-59477-133-0 (pbk.)
  ISBN-10: 1-59477-133-2 (pbk.)
  1. Religion and science. 2. Astronomy—Religious aspects—Christianity. 3. Mythology, Dogon. 4. Astronomy, Dogon. I. Title.
  BL253.S37 2006
  299.6'83—dc22

                                                          2006017865

Printed and bound in the United States

10   9   8

Text design by Priscilla Baker
Text layout by Virginia Scott Bowman
This book was typeset in Sabon and Agenda with Schneidler Initials and Agenda as the display typefaces

To send correspondence to the author of this book, mail a first-class letter to the author c/o Inner Traditions • Bear & Company, One Park Street, Rochester, VT 05767, and we will forward the communication.

The Author and Publisher wish to thank the following for permission to use their excerpted material in this book:

"Interior illustrations" by Ron Miller, from *A Brief History of Time* by Stephen W. Hawking, copyright © 1988, 1996 by Stephen W. Hawking. Used by permission of Bantam Books, a division of Random House, Inc.

Selections from *Codes of Evolution* by Rush W. Dozier Jr., copyright © 1992 by Rush W. Dozier Jr. Used by permission of Crown Publishers, a division of Random House, Inc.

Selections from *Gods and Symbols of Ancient Mexico and the Maya* by Mary Miller and Karl Taube, copyright © 1993 Thames & Hudson Ltd., London. Reprinted by permission of Thames & Hudson, Inc.

Selections reprinted by permission of the publisher from *Judaism in the First Centuries of the Christian Era: Volume 1—The Age of Tannaim* by George Foot Moore, Cambridge, MA: Harvard University Press, copyright © 1927, 1930 by the President and Fellows of Harvard College

Selections reprinted from *Myth and Symbol in Ancient Egypt* by R. T. Rundle Clark, copyright © 1959 Thames & Hudson Ltd., London. Reprinted by permission of Thames & Hudson, Inc.

Selections reprinted from *Mythology* by Edith Hamilton copyright © 1942 by Edith Hamilton; copyright © renewed 1969 by Dorian Fielding Reid and Doris Fielding Reid. used by permission of Little, Brown and Company, Inc.

Selections reprinted from *The Orion Mystery* by Robert Bauval and Adrian Gilbert, copyright © 1994 by Robert Bauval and Adrian Gilbert. Used by permission of Crown Publishers, a division of Random House, Inc.

Selections and diagrams reprinted from *The Pale Fox* by Marcel Griaule and Germaine Dieterlen, copyright © 1986 by The Continuum Foundation, permission requested of Afrikan World Books, PO Box 16447, Baltimore, MD 21217

Selections reprinted from Serge Sauneron, David Lorton (trans.), *The Priests of Ancient Egypt*, copyright © 2000 by Cornell University. Used by permission of the publisher, Cornell University Press.

For Ogotemmeli, Marcel Griaule,
and Germaine Dieterlen

CONTENTS

FOREWORD

This book—small in size, large in significance—proves that the very latest scientific work on the structure and genesis of matter, quantum theory, and possibly both string and torsion theory was known in very ancient times. However, it was (and in certain cases still is) expressed in myth and symbol rather than in mathematical formulas.

Laird Scranton's research speaks eloquently and remarkably for itself. No advanced technical knowledge is needed to follow his arguments. To appreciate what is at stake, a brief discussion of the obstacles this work must face may prove useful.

———

Because the history of just about everything is written by the winners, it is invariably difficult to gauge, to judge, sometimes even to know, that a battle has taken place or that one is under way. The winners are at liberty to distort, misrepresent, or ignore all that does not support their "official" version, and so they do. It is this version that is disseminated in schools and through the mainstream media. As a result the public gets, and generally accepts at face value, what it has been taught.

Sometimes this doesn't matter much. If we are ignorant of the actual arguments that were once put forward by defenders of the flat earth theory, we are scarcely the poorer for it. However, in other instances, unquestioning acceptance of the winners' tale may carry serious adverse consequences.

The accepted history of human civilization is one such winners' tale, the history of science another. Today, on a daily basis, through every media outlet, we witness a world spinning out of control. This should be obvious to everyone. Able commentators analyze menacing, possibly irreversible, trends from every quarter and angle: environmental, ecological, economic, medical, military, political, sociological. Such trends include global warming, irreversible pollution, looming epidemics, peak oil, development of weapons of mass destruction, nuclear proliferation, overpopulation. . . . The litany is endless, familiar, and numbingly repetitious. Yet beneath the racket, subaudibly and never openly articulated (because it is considered self-evident), a comforting ostinato sounds.

We are endlessly assured by history and by science (and therefore by and large we believe) that despite all those looming doomsday scenarios, we of the twenty-first century represent the most advanced, most developed, and most highly evolved human beings ever to inhabit the planet. No one has been taught anything seriously contrary to these beliefs in high school or university; nothing in our most respected Western mainstream media organs (e.g., *New York Times*, *Scientific American*, *National Geographic*) would suggest an alternative to, or reconsideration of, our firmly entrenched historical and scientific winners' tale—although even these sources routinely publish articles from archaeology, archaeoastronomy, and other subdisciplines devoted to the past that, put together, would suggest that a comprehensive reconsideration is in order.

Because progress as a linear phenomenon (starting in a misty, primitive, prehistoric past and leading in direct, linear fashion—give or take a blip or detour here and there—to our advanced, developed, and evolved selves) is the central tenet of our reigning "Church of Progress," no such reconsideration will come from within the winners' ranks.

———

This does not mean that a reconsideration of the march of progress cannot come from without; victory is one thing, subduing the entire territory quite another. In fact, a succession of guerilla scholars have challenged the accepted progressive scenario almost from the beginning of its establishment as dogma in the mid-nineteenth century, which is when modern science rolled into high gear and when our standard Western version of history was developed.

In a nutshell, history sees civilization as an essentially white, Eurocentric process, beginning with ancient Greece. Anything prior to the classic Greek period, or taking place elsewhere on the planet, did not count as "civilization," although the Greeks themselves readily acknowledged their own debt to the earlier culture of Egypt. Moreover, in Europe, up to the mid-nineteenth century, it was generally accepted by scholars of all persuasions (as a matter of tradition, if not fact) that Egypt, not Greece, was the fount of a high and very ancient science. Moreover, the legends and mythologies from societies virtually everywhere in the world routinely reference long-lost, sophisticated civilizations that disappeared, often under catastrophic circumstances (the Old Testament deluge may be the best known). However, none of this was given credence by the priesthood of the victorious Church of Progress, although, in retrospect, some early challengers were presenting serious evidence for the alternative, older view (e.g., Ignatius Donnelly's best-selling *Atlantis* and astronomer Norman Lockyer's proposal that Stonehenge was an astronomical instrument). Any suggestion that an advanced, exact science existed in the distant past was attacked as heresy or dismissed and derided as fantasy.

It was not until the second half of the twentieth century that guerilla scholarship became a noticeable, if uncoordinated, force—in part because television and the cinema do not feel obligated to stick to establishment academic guidelines. They are interested in profit, not paradigms. Although they were often dumbed-down and sensationalized, alternative viewpoints from a spectrum of disciplines began reaching and exciting mass audiences.

Meanwhile, on the scholarly front, challenging solid evidence was piling up. Beginning with *Hamlet's Mill* by two historians of science at the Massachusetts Institute of Technology, Giorgio de Santillana and Hertha von Dechend, archaeoastronomy became a subdiscipline in its own right, demonstrating that a sophisticated astronomy preceded recorded history and stretched back into the remotest past. A magisterial, elaborately documented reformulation of the sacred science of ancient Egypt, *The Temple of Man* by R. A. Schwaller de Lubicz, put scholarly teeth into that long-lived European conviction of Egypt as the original fount of ancient wisdom. *The Tao of Physics* by physicist Fritjof Capra drew convincing parallels between ancient Vedic cosmological tradition and contemporary physics. My own geological investigation into the water-weathering pattern on the Great Sphinx of Giza (supported and elaborated upon by geologist Robert M. Schoch) supplied another powerful scientific verification of the lost civilization hypothesis.

During the past two decades, despite the fierce opposition or studied neglect of the establishment, major and compelling contributions to this body of evidence have proliferated; some adding valuable pieces to already established knowledge, some opening up whole new vistas. *The Science of the Dogon* falls mainly into the latter category. It demonstrates in unequivocal fashion not only that the cosmologies of the little Dogon tribe of West Africa and of the ancient Egyptians are essentially the same but also, more importantly, that these cosmologies are effectively identical to the latest findings of contemporary physics.

In other words, the most advanced science we now have at our disposal was known at least as far back as the beginnings of ancient Egypt and was also available to a supposedly primitive, remote, and isolated African tribe with no demonstrable contact with ancient Egypt. Scranton also finds parallel instances of the same ancient science cropping up in all manner of unexpected and unrelated traditions. Taken altogether, the evidence seems overwhelming and beyond dispute.

Because there is good reason to believe that the entire Egyptian doctrine is a legacy from a still earlier (and unknown) civilization, everything held sacred regarding the development of civilization by our Church of Progress has to be radically revised and rethought from the ground up. We are not who we think we are.

The Science of the Dogon provides a unique window into the distant past and perhaps the opportunity to discover who we once were—keepers of a science no less sophisticated than our own, yet with a very different and far more benign relationship to our planet. It is just possible that the key to salvaging our own future lies in an understanding of that nature.

It would be difficult to imagine a more significant contribution to the advancement of science than *The Science of the Dogon*. It will be very interesting to see what kind of reception awaits this extraordinary book.

JOHN ANTHONY WEST

John Anthony West is an independent Egyptologist who has studied and written about ancient Egypt since 1986. His controversial work on redating the Great Sphinx has challenged long-accepted notions of Egyptian history. He is the author of *Serpent in the Sky* and *The Traveler's Key to Ancient Egypt* and often leads tours to Egypt as a guide and lecturer.

ACKNOWLEDGMENTS

This book would not have been possible without the support and help of friends and family. In particular, I would like to thank my wife Risa, son Isaac, and daughter Hannah for their support and patience. I am also very grateful for the generous support, encouragement, and friendship of Teresa Vergani, whose insights into Dogon symbols have been a great help. I would like to thank John Anthony West for writing the foreword to this book, and for his generous and unflagging support of my work and that of other like-minded authors. I am also indebted to Doug Kenyon at *Atlantis Rising* magazine for printing a related article of mine on Dogon symbols, and to Martin Gray for the use of his beautiful photograph to illustrate that same article. I have greatly appreciated the enthusiasm and support of Ida Moffett Harrison and Stephen C. Infantino, whose careful work on *The Pale Fox* has proved so pivotal to my effort, and I wish to thank Mr. Nataki at African World Books in Baltimore for generously allowing me to quote from that work. I would also like to thank the many friends and family members who have allowed me to use them as sounding boards for my ideas (sometimes against their will), including Lynda Falkenstein, Sue and Howard Sherer, Will Newman and Sue Clark, David and Kathy Scranton, Cathy Agnello Brown, Madeleine Bohrer, John Gardenier, Bill Churchman, Eric Infante, Dave Zimmer, Doris Schwaller, all of the ladies at Monroe Pediatrics, Desiree and Andre Krueger, Bill Przylucki, Jason Colavito, Helene Hagan, Michael Sherer, Raffi Arenos, and my mother Peg Scranton for proofreading and commenting on early drafts of my manuscript. Last but not least, to cousin Harvey Kornit—many psychic thanks for the copy of *Ancient Near Eastern Texts*.

INTRODUCTION

This book is first and foremost about resemblances—those between myths of different ancient cultures around the world, between the cultures' ritual practices, and between the interpretations that such cultures placed on mythological symbols and words. The pervasive nature of these resemblances suggests a relationship between the cultures themselves—from Africa, India, and the Near East to the Americas, Polynesia, Japan, and China—a relationship perhaps defined first by what appears to be a common system of myth.

One might reasonably ask how early societies from such widespread regions could have acquired a common mythological system. Although it is not within the scope of this volume to compare the various competing academic theories that have been proposed to explain this phenomenon, common sense tells us that there are only a few reasonable ways in which it could have happened. The system could have developed first in one region, then migrated to the others, or it could have grown up independently in all regions based on some innate psychological aspect of human beings that leads them to express themselves through similar myths and symbols. A third possibility—one that is dismissed as unreasonable in the prevailing academic view, but one that is actually put forth in the traditions of some early societies—is the notion of myth as a planned societal system, deliberately disseminated by capable, knowledgeable teachers.

If we were to suspend disbelief for a moment and allow the possibility of such a deliberately designed system of myth, and if we could somehow unearth a substantially intact version of that system, then our thesis would imply that there should be an underlying logic to the system, including its themes, symbols, and words, that we could overtly demonstrate. If this hypothetical system had, in fact, been deliberately taught around the globe at some point in antiquity, then we should find evidence of this same underlying logical plan in the myths of different world cultures.

The impulse to write this book came out of the discovery—made possible by the long-term, careful studies of two French anthropologists—of just such a well-preserved system in the myths of the Dogon of Mali. The Dogon are a modern-day African tribal people who live along the cliffs of the Bandiagara escarpment, south of the Sahara Desert, near Timbuktu and not far from the Niger River in Mali, West Africa. The tribe consists of approximately 100,000 individuals distributed among some 700 villages. Although the origins of the Dogon people are not certain, by their own reckoning they arrived at their current location during the fourteenth or fifteenth century, after having migrated from a previous home along the Niger River, perhaps as a way of avoiding conversion to Islam. They are an agricultural people known for their artwork—especially their carved wooden gate locks, granary doors, and masks.[1]

Many different aspects of Dogon culture suggest a long history for the tribe. Perhaps the most suggestive of these is its possession of a detailed set of esoteric cosmogonic myths and mythological traditions comparable to those that are known to have existed in ancient Egypt 5,000 years ago. Also highly suggestive of an ancient lineage for the Dogon people are their religious rituals and practices, which in key ways mirror those of Judaism, an ancient religion that is known to date from this same remote period. Furthermore, the Dogon myths are expressed in words and symbols that are shared commonly with the Amazigh, the tribes of hunters who lived in Egypt prior to the beginning of the First Egyptian Dynasty. Perhaps most significantly, Dogon cosmology is documented in tribal drawings that often take the same shape as the ancient pictograms used to produce Egyptian hieroglyphic writing.

It will be my goal in this book to outline a broad set of classical and mythological themes, symbols, and storylines set forth by the Dogon myths, to use well-documented Dogon symbolic definitions to illuminate an organizational structure for the myths, which are seemingly based on knowledge of modern science, and to demonstrate that evidence of this same symbolic system survives in fragments of other world mythologies. Although some will think it absurd to suggest that the people of 3400 BC were learning theories of advanced science at a time when they hardly had mastered the skills of stone masonry, what is believable is that the structures of civilizing knowledge were presented to mankind in a form that would orient us toward a larger understanding of the sciences and that generous hints about the origins of the universe, the composition of matter, and the reproductive processes of life were incorporated within this framework. These hints were couched in terms that primitive people would be likely to recognize as their knowledge and abilities improved.

During this discussion, I will focus on similar mythological words and symbols that are found in ancient cultures from around the world and on the interpretations these cultures place on such symbols. From the outset, it is important to note that, from an academic viewpoint, a simple resemblance between words—say, two words with somewhat similar pronunciation and meaning—is not an adequate foundation upon which to infer a true relationship between the words. Rather, what is required is some additional level of corroborating evidence—for example, a second level of meaning tagged to both words or a ritual shape associated with both words. Also, in this text, when I refer to two words from different cultures as being related, I do not necessarily mean to imply a strict linguistic lineage for the words. Rather, when two similarly pronounced words carry the same multiple meanings or share a single well-defined meaning that can be corroborated by other evidence, I will consider the words to be related within the context of what seems to be a larger symbolic system. Likewise, the concurrence of several similarly pronounced words of comparable meaning, taken in the same mythological context, also will be considered to justify the suspicion of a direct mythological connection between the words.

As we proceed, we will see the important role played by resemblances between words when interpreting the meanings of myth. Such resemblances often begin with similarities of pronunciation and in many cases involve classic homonyms—words like *their* and *there*, which are pronounced alike but carry different meanings. However, when working with ancient written languages where vowel sounds were implied but not written—as is the case with ancient Hebrew or Egyptian hieroglyphs— the definition of a homonym must necessarily stretch to allow for differences in vowel sound interpolation by different translators.

For example, if written English words omitted vowel sounds, then the words *their* and *there* would both be written *thr*. If, like ancient Egyptian hieroglyphs, the actual pronunciations of these words were no longer certain, one translator might defend *ther* as a proper spelling while another might prefer *thear*. In situations analogous to these I ask readers to "tune" their perceptions to hear the underlying resemblances of pronunciation and consider such words to be homonyms of each other—which at heart the original English words actually are. Also, in English, certain letters can carry phonetic values that are similar to each other, like the letter K and the "hard" C sound or the letter S and the "soft" C sound. Similar situations exist among the thousands of Egyptian glyph characters, so we often find two Egyptian words pronounced the same way but written with different glyphs. By English standards, these Egyptian words qualify as true homonyms—much like the English words *ceiling* and *sealing*. In other cases we will encounter Dogon words that seem to be direct counterparts of Egyptian words, even though the pronunciation appears to have changed over a long period of time. For instance, we will argue that the Dogon word *ogo* is essentially the same as the Egyptian word *aakhu* and that the name of the Dogon Sigui festival correlates to the Egyptian word *skhai*, meaning "celebration or festival." Again, acknowledgment of the phonetic resemblances between these words rests on a kind of perceptual leniency on the part of the reader. In my view, such flexibility constitutes a kind of legitimate permissiveness that must be applied in order to properly understand real relationships between Dogon and Egyptian words and so will be reflected throughout this study in our use of the term *homonym*. The reader should also be aware that the prevalence of these kinds of homonyms as separate word entries in the Egyptian hieroglyphic dictionary can often produce multiple and varied meanings for a single pronunciation—a situation that, when combined with similar Dogon multiple word meanings, often helps us to substantiate correlations between specific Dogon and Egyptian words.

When I talk about symbols in this study, the intention is that the reader will infer his or her own broad sense of what constitutes a symbol based on examples of symbolism in Dogon culture and mythology. Among the Dogon, simple acts of daily life, such as the weaving of a cloth or the plowing of a field, might carry important symbolism. Seemingly insignificant details, such as the order in which tasks are performed or the number of years between ritual observances, might also carry symbolism. For the reader to fully understand the breadth and depth of this kind of societal symbolism, he or she must begin to adopt the larger mindset that seems to govern the assignment of symbolism in both the Dogon and Egyptian systems. Within this mindset, such subtle aspects of existence as the shape that a dog's mouth forms when it barks, the tendency of a rabbit to tremble, or the design of a woven basket can all be used to convey symbolic meaning. Integral to this mindset (and contrary to the modern academic prejudice against the significance of simple resemblance between different words) is the Dogon assumption that similarities of pronunciation imply a symbolic relationship between words. It is consistent with this mindset, for example, that the Dogon word *ogo* (which I will show symbolizes the concept of light) forms the root of the words *hogon* (a Dogon priestly title), *Ogotemmeli* (the name of a Dogon priest), and the word *Dogon* itself.

For the purposes of understanding Dogon myths and culture, this study relies on the works of Marcel Griaule and Germaine Dieterlen, two French anthropologists who lived among the Dogon in the 1930s, 1940s, and 1950s and documented their customs and rituals. Griaule and Dieterlen recorded their observations about the Dogon in four principal works, to which there are references throughout this study. The first is a book titled *Conversations with Ogotemmeli*, a journal of Griaule's thirty-three-day introduction to the Dogon religion by a knowledgeable Dogon priest. The second is a finished study of the Dogon religion called *The Pale Fox*, which was completed by by Dieterlen after Griaule's death. The third is an article by Griaule and Dieterlen that discusses Dogon religious knowledge relating to the star system of Sirius, titled "A Sudanese Sirius System." The last is an article written by Griaule and Dieterlen titled "The Dogon," which is included in *African Worlds*, an anthology of articles by various authors about the cosmologies of African tribes. A fifth text—a dictionary of the Dogon language called the *Dictionnaire Dogon*, which was compiled by Genevieve Calame-Griaule, Griaule's daughter—will be another source of references to Dogon words.

The authenticity of what Griaule and Dieterlen documented as Dogon cosmology has been recently called into question by anthropologists such as Walter Van Beek, who studied the tribe in the 1980s and 1990s. Van Beek found no evidence of a native Dogon cosmology and concluded that the obliging Dogon priests simply invented their stories to satisfy the insistent questions of Griaule. However, this study will point out many esoteric similarities between Dogon mythological and cosmological symbols and words, as reported by Griaule, and those of ancient Egypt that are consistent with other known Dogon and Egyptian cultural similarities. The extent and depth of these similarities all but preclude the possibility that Dogon cosmology as presented by the Dogon priests could have been the product of casual invention.

Egyptian hieroglyphs provide us with a unique method for validating linguistic and conceptual similarities. One hallmark of Egyptian hieroglyphs is that they remained remarkably unchanged in form from their first appearance around 3000 BC to their last use some 3,000 years later. Although many new glyphs, or characters, were added during that period of time, the form and grammar of hieroglyphic writing remained so remarkably constant that an Egyptian scribe working in 700 BC would have been quite able to read and understand an inscription written 2,000 years earlier. Moreover, hieroglyphic writing conveyed meaning on two levels at the same time. The hieroglyphic characters combined to form words, much like the letters of an alphabet. However, the pictures used to draw the hieroglyphic phrases often lent additional nuances of meaning to the words, much like the combination of images and subtitles when watching a foreign movie. What this means is that, even if a given Egyptian word evolved in meaning over thousands of years, we might still find traces of an original meaning in the hieroglyphic characters that were used to express it. It should be noted here that, unless otherwise specifically stated, all references in this work to Egyptian hieroglyphs, their forms, and their meanings were taken from *An Egyptian Hieroglyphic Dictionary* by Sir E. A. Wallis Budge.

The choice in this study to base comparisons of Dogon and Egyptian words on Budge's dictionary is one that might not be understood by the traditional Egyptologist. In the years since Budge's dictionary was compiled, the study of Egyptian hieroglyphic writing has moved beyond Budge in several respects. This stems primarily from disagreements of scholarship and differences of opinion about the proper pronunciation of Egyptian words. However, for the present purposes, the choice to use Budge's dictionary is driven by purely practical considerations. An example of such a consideration—which, as we will see, repeats in similar form for many key words relating to Dogon cosmology—is illustrated by the word for dung beetle, which, by the currently accepted view of Egyptian language, should be written *hpr*. Budge's dictionary lists the word as *kheper*. Among the Dogon, the word *ke* refers to the dung beetle in specific and to the larger class of water beetles in general. Like the root word *kheper*, which for Budge implies the concepts of nonexistence and existence, the Dogon word *ke* forms the root of words implying the "organization of creation." As a researcher hoping to compare two sets of cosmological words, I found myself faced with a critical choice—whether to rely on the prevailing view of the Egyptian language, in which no relationship between Dogon and Egyptian words is apparent, or to rely on Budge's dictionary, where clear relationships between the words, pronunciations, and meanings are obvious. While the suggestive examples presented in this volume might not be sufficient to fully substantiate the choice to use Budge's dictionary, my intention is to support this choice with a second volume devoted to the many relationships between key Dogon cosmological words and Egyptian words, based on Budge. It is my belief that knowledge of Egyptian hieroglyphic writing alone is not a sufficient credential to establish a person's ability to judge the usefulness of Budge's dictionary in relation to Dogon words. Although traditional Egyptologists might feel justified in questioning this choice based on professional experience, they should also consider whether their own background in Dogon cosmology and language (or lack thereof) actually qualifies them to defend this stance. I leave it to professional Egyptologists to explain how a dictionary as much-maligned as Budge's could predictively describe the meanings and pronunciations of words from a culture as similar to that of ancient Egypt as the Dogon's.

ONE

HOW THIS BOOK CAME TO BE

The unusual subject matter of this book might lead some to wonder how I came to write it. This is especially true because I am not an anthropologist, I never pursued a serious study of archaeology or astrophysics in school, I have never visited Africa or Egypt, and prior to this research, I was not well versed in ancient languages. By profession I am a software designer who specializes in writing custom computer programs for businesses. What this means in terms of my daily job is that I am paid to interpret, understand, and maintain old computer programs and to design and write new programs for a wide variety of companies. The professional skill set that I have acquired while performing my job might seem distantly removed from the study of ancient religious symbols because my job is sometimes a highly technical one and ancient religions would appear by definition to be inherently primitive. In fact, if you believe that the stories and symbols of most ancient religions evolved without intentional design over many hundreds or thousands of years, then it is debatable whether my professional skills would have any bearing at all on the subject. On the other hand, if you imagine for a moment that any given religious symbol—for example, a character used to write a hieroglyphic word—was specifically chosen to represent its meaning, then my software design skills start to come into play because one of the most common tasks while writing a computer program involves the deliberate selection of symbols to represent concepts.

For one programmer to successfully maintain the work of another, he or she must first learn to identify the intended meanings of the other programmer's symbols. A good software designer also learns over time to incorporate clues to the meaning of a symbol into the form of the symbol itself. For instance, if a variable in a program is meant to represent an invoice number, the symbol will be easier for another programmer to understand if it is called "INVNO" than if it is called "XYZ123." When interpreting a program, if the starting point is merely an abstract group of characters—like the letters "STXPCT"—then there could be endless possibilities for what the symbol actually represents. However, if you can eventually place the letters into a context—for instance, if you realize that the field name "STXPCT" is meant to represent the words "state tax percent"—then the challenge of interpreting the program and its purpose becomes much, much easier.

Computer programs are often modified and therefore are subject to change over time. Sometimes a programmer encounters several different copies of what started out as the same program and must try to make sense of different versions. Years ago I developed a programming tool to help me identify and resolve these differences. It prints a side-by-side list of the components of two programs, comparing each line in one program to its counterpart in the other. Lines that have no exact counterpart are printed in boldface. The finished printout provides me with a template for comparing the versions. Any line printed in regular typeface is most likely a part of the original program. Those printed in boldface were most likely added to one program or removed from the other sometime after the original program was written. Sometimes a programmer's comment in one version provides information that explains some obscure aspect of another version. Ancient creation stories present us with substantially this same situation; they appear to represent alternate versions of what might have once been a single story or system of stories. My initial approach to this study was to use what is essentially a programming technique to provide a conceptual framework for understanding the stories by grouping the similarities and highlighting the differences between different myths.

When I began my research for this book in 1993, I thought I was simply reading for pleasure. I had purchased a book called *Unexplained* by Jerome Clark, a well-known investigator of anomalous claims, that includes chapters on a variety of intriguing unsolved mysteries. One of these chapters is devoted to a summary of Robert K. G. Temple's work *The Sirius Mystery,* and it piqued my interest so much that I ordered Temple's book. His discussion of the Dogon tribe and their roots, as he perceived them, in ancient Egypt fit nicely with other recreational reading I had done relating to the pyramids and the Sphinx. I was also interested in the parallels between Dogon rituals and those of modern-day Judaism because the Dogon religion includes enticing explanations for the practice of circumcision and the celebration of the jubilee year. I began to let my new reading be guided by sources referenced in Temple's book.

Like many students of ancient religions, my research led me in a variety of directions. I read many books on subjects that were directly related to my topic, such as the emergence of the Egyptian and Sumerian civilizations and the mythologies of Mesopotamia. However, questions arose as a consequence of those readings that led me to subjects that were of less obvious value to my main interests. I found myself studying the history of calendars, the origins of the alphabet, and the evolution of numbers. I felt that I needed to know more about basic modern astronomy and the astronomy of the ancients. It seemed helpful to acquaint myself with the creation stories of various modern religions and the symbols and gods that they celebrate. During this same period, I also continued to pursue what I thought was purely recreational reading. For instance, I read *A Brief History of Time* by Stephen Hawking and Immanuel Velikovsky's *Worlds in Collision* and *Ages in Chaos.*

Later I happened across a reference to Marcel Griaule's book *Conversations with Ogotemmeli* and ordered it through a bookstore. Although it is a short book, it provided me with a firsthand account of the Dogon religion and an introduction to the Dogon mythological mindset. After reading it I began to see many parallels between Dogon mythology, Egyptian mythology, and Judaism. For instance, I could see that the granary resembled the pyramid and that the ram symbol of the Dogon might be related to the ram's horn of Judaism that is sounded at Rosh Hashanah. I had learned that the pyramid of Egypt represented a star, that the Dogon religion centered on the two stars of Sirius, and that the Star of David in Judaism consisted of two interlocked pyramids—or in Egyptian symbolic terms, two stars.

Many of my sources provided fragmentary references to ancient tablets from Egypt and Sumer, and in some cases I wished that I could read translations of the full texts. One book relating to Old Testament documents that I was actively seeking but unable to find (this was prior to online searches for out-of-print books) was James Bennett Pritchard's *Ancient Near Eastern Texts.* I had just exhausted all of the possible local sources for the book when a box appeared at my back door. One of my wife's elderly cousins had coincidentally decided to clean house and, knowing of our love of books, packed up a box of them to send to us. Although he had no knowledge of my interest in ancient religions, he included among them Pritchard's *Ancient Near Eastern Texts.*

One lesson I only learned over time was to question the consensus wisdom of mainstream reference sources. When I expanded my search for parallels of Dogon mythology to Sumerian religion, I read and believed any number of dictionaries of mythology, all of which agreed that the earliest gods of the Sumerian creation tradition were An, Enlil, and Enki. I had hoped to find a match for the Nummo of Dogon tradition but was resigned to concede that I would not find it—until I read Annie Caubet and Patrick Pouyssegur's book *The Ancient Near East,* which explained about an earlier mother goddess called Nammu. Even now I actively seek out alternate sources of information on any topic that is of importance to me—especially those of eighteenth- and nineteenth-century writers whose views were not colored by modern academic preferences—in the fervent hope that each author might include some new tidbit of information that suddenly completes some unfinished puzzle for me.

When I first realized that I was pursuing a goal with my research,

I thought that it was simply to define the attributes of what I saw as an "original" creation story—one that included shared elements of the Sumerian, Akkadian, Babylonian, Egyptian, and Dogon traditions. I could see that there were enough common elements to suggest that these traditions had all evolved from a single source. I understood that the quest to identify these similarities might bring with it other new insights into the earliest creation traditions, but that possibility seemed like icing on the cake rather than an ultimate goal to be sought. The scattered symbols and stories that appeared to tie these ancient mythologies together were by no means complete enough to make any kind of overall sense.

Late in the 1990s I acquired a copy of *The Pale Fox*, the English translation of Griaule and Dieterlen's anthropological study of the Dogon. The detail it provided about Dogon religious symbols and mythology was frankly overwhelming. I could see that the Dogon stories seemed to be speaking in metaphor, but based on my limited experience with Dogon symbols, the metaphors were in no way decipherable. What I did come away with after reading it was a clear, professional sense that the symbols had been deliberately designed, but for me they were still just random symbols without a context. Studying them was like watching a foreign movie without subtitles—it was possible to get an overall sense of purpose and direction but not much more. Years later I was to make contact with Dr. Stephen C. Infantino, the Humboldt State University professor who had translated the English edition of *The Pale Fox*. He mentioned that he had suspected during the translation that the Dogon creation story might represent more than mere tribal myths.

Based on a suggestion in Temple's book, I purchased and began to study Sir E. A. Wallis Budge's *An Egyptian Hieroglyphic Dictionary*, trying to develop a sense of how the hieroglyphic language was constructed. In some cases, the specific characters used to form a hieroglyphic word seemed to directly describe the word. For instance, an entry for the word *good* consists of a picture of a mother and a baby—very much like the Chinese pictogram for "good." However, in other cases there seemed to be no obvious relationship between the hieroglyphic characters and the concept conveyed by the word. I also began to read studies of other primitive mythologies, including the book *Alpha: The Myths of Creation* by Charles H. Long, which summarizes many different creation traditions.

In January 2000, I stumbled upon a clue that was to prove to be the key that would unlock many doors for me in my understanding of Dogon symbolism. The pivotal event was figuratively a repetition of Helen Keller's discovery of language. I was struggling with the most obvious theme of the Dogon creation story—the recurring references to water. I had just reread Griaule's quotations from Ogotemmeli about the nature of water and was perusing an *Encyclopedia Britannica* article on water, trying to recount the most basic scientific facts and attributes of water. I happened across a series of sentences that seemed very familiar to me, even though I was reading them for the first time. It occurred to me that the words were familiar because they restated, almost verbatim, one of Griaule's quotations from Ogotemmeli. I compared the passages and verified that they indeed nearly matched. The parallel nature of the sentences seemed more than coincidental, and it made me wonder if the Dogon creation story was somehow a mask for what was essentially encyclopedic information about water. If so, then I had possibly discovered the missing clue I most desperately needed—a context within which to interpret the Dogon symbols.

I began to review the events of the Dogon, Sumerian, and Egyptian creation stories, looking specifically for information about water, and what I found were metaphors for each of the significant scientific attributes of water—its molecular structure, its three physical states, and each of the stages of the natural water cycle. More importantly, I realized that if I used the encyclopedia article on water as a guide and simply followed its main points, it outlined for me the corresponding elements that I was to find in the Dogon creation story. This discovery changed the entire nature of my approach to understanding the episodes of Dogon mythology presented in *The Pale Fox*. Suddenly I devoted my effort to the task of understanding the context of each episode, hoping to find a much-needed shortcut for interpreting the meaning of each one.

My success in relating the encyclopedia article on water to the symbols and events of the Dogon creation story led me to examine similarities between Dogon symbols and the science of human reproduction. I was astounded to discover that I could again follow the major topics of a related encyclopedia article and find similar themes within the Dogon creation story. I began to see the creation story itself as a kind of encyclopedia of information and found myself turning again and again to modern encyclopedia articles to help interpret it.

What followed during the next year were almost daily insights into the meanings of the symbols that I had been studying for the prior five years. Each evening I would come home from work with a target list of words and concepts to explore in the hieroglyphic dictionary, testing the boundaries of correspondence between the Egyptian and Dogon creation traditions. My wife, Risa, and I subscribe to a thin weekly magazine called *Science News,* which provides a brief summary of the week's events in science. As often as not, when I read it I learned some new fact from the leading edge of science that conformed to or confirmed some aspect of Dogon mythology. My family and friends tolerated my growing preoccupation with the subject and offered suggestions that sometimes proved to be quite helpful. My wife's insights into Judaism and knowledge of Hebrew were of great help on many occasions, and my son and daughter often reported helpful details that they had learned in school about topics relating to mine. One afternoon my daughter excitedly recognized a Dogon drawing as a representation of chromosomes and spindles, based on diagrams she had seen in her high school biology class. My son made the connection between the Dogon numerological assignments of the numbers four and three as male and female and the number of branches in the X and Y chromosomes.

At this point in my understanding, it struck me as rather far-fetched that an ancient creation story could be conveying information about subjects like the quantum structure of an atom. So, for a period of time, I consciously discarded clues such as references to pellets of clay and spiraling coils—possible metaphors for particles and waves—simply because I did not believe that a myth could be leading me in the direction of quantum theory. By February 2000, I realized that I had acquired insights worth writing about and that I was ready to compose what I expected would be a twenty-page article, to simply record what I had learned. Because I was still actively learning about my subject as I wrote, the first draft took a journal-like form, listing each new revelation as I discovered it—some of them pertinent and some not. After several weeks, the article had reached forty pages, and I believed that I had exhausted all that I would ever have to say on the subject.

The Dogon images of particles and waves continued their nagging insistence, so I decided to reread Stephen Hawking's *A Brief History of Time*. By this point my understanding of Dogon and Egyptian mythological symbols had come along far enough that I recognized several of Hawking's descriptions and diagrams as counterparts to familiar entries in *The Pale Fox*. I was able to identify the shape of Hawking's diagram of the event horizon of a black hole as Amma's egg and his description of the four categories of quantum particles as the Dogon drawing of the germination of the *sene*. These discoveries convinced me not only that I was on the right track in my analysis of Dogon mythological symbols but also that whatever source originally composed these myths knew more about the fundamental aspects of science than I did. From that point forward, I quietly assumed the role of student and the Dogon creation story became the teacher.

I was still left with important details, symbols, and diagrams from *The Pale Fox* that I felt were related to the structure of matter but that I could not understand. Since the Dogon symbols had thus far led me to details of atomic and quantum structure, I decided to educate myself about the science of string theory and purchased *The Elegant Universe* by Brian Greene. One evening a diagram in the book that depicted the vibratory patterns of strings stopped me dead in my tracks. I realized that I was staring at the very image of one of the Dogon drawings that had eluded my understanding. After that I was not the least bit surprised to find that the remainder of Greene's book confirmed item after item in Griaule and Dieterlen's anthropological study.

Once my correlations had been made between Dogon myth and modern science, the next step was to test my own initial theory—that the Dogon and Egyptian cosmologies represent two versions of the same original tradition. If my interpretation of the Dogon symbols and their scientific meanings was correct, then I should find evidence of the same science in the Egyptian myths and symbols. I concluded that a key source for finding this evidence was the hieroglyphic dictionary.

As it turns out, the initial impulse to compare Dogon and Egyptian symbols was a fortuitous one because the unchanged nature of the Egyptian hieroglyphs provided me with a reliable tool for correlating the underlying scientific meanings of Egyptian words with those of the Dogon. My intention had always been to learn to read and write Egyptian hieroglyphs. However, at this point in my research, a lack of formal study of the language actually proved to be an asset because it freed me to infer likely meanings for various symbols without the prejudice of current academically preferred meanings. I should emphasize that when in doubt, I have presumed that the interpretive work on Egyptian hieroglyphic language that has been done by many respected scholars over many years is correct. Still, one finds frequent references in ancient sources to a secret language of the Egyptian priests—much like the secret priestly language of the Dogon—and so for me, the possibility of alternate meanings for any given hieroglyphic character or word falls well within the realm of believability. This is especially true when the proposed new meaning succeeds in reconnecting the characters of the hieroglyphic word to the concept that the word expresses.

In 2001, I read a mathematical analysis of Dogon symbols called "Ethnomathematics and Symbolic Thought: The Culture of the Dogon" by Teresa Vergani, a French mathematician, artist, and poet from Portugal. I had been looking for someone with knowledge of Dogon symbols who might be interested in discussing my manuscript. Vergani's article clearly demonstrated her familiarity with and fondness for Dogon mythology, so I decided to contact her and ask if she would consider reviewing a draft of my text. She most generously agreed, then read what I had written and offered her insights and suggestions. To my benefit, what started as only a distant professional contact has now turned into a most important and valuable friendship.

Another turning point in my study came in March and April of 2002, when I again focused my attention on the details of string theory. I purchased a book called *The Matter Myth* by Paul Davies and John Gribbin, which presented several diagrams relating to string theory. Of particular interest to me was a diagram that illustrated two types of simple string intersections whose shapes seemed somehow familiar. At about the same time, I had begun to explore the hieroglyphic characters used in various forms of the Egyptian word *ntt* (to weave)—the creative skill used by the goddess Neith when she created matter. The first two examples presented in Budge's dictionary were spelled using glyphs whose shapes matched each of the diagrams of the two simple string intersections. This discovery quickly led me to review the various spellings of the name Neith itself. I found that one form of the goddess's name was written using a glyph that closely matched a diagram of the complex string interaction.

There were still a series of diagrams from *The Pale Fox* that seemed to relate to the behavior of strings but whose significance had eluded me for several years. These diagrams show the seven evolutions of the vibrations within what the Dogon call *po* (smallest grain). My success at finding validation for concepts of string theory in hieroglyphs spurred me to look again for scientific counterparts to the Dogon diagrams. This time what I found was a specific discussion of the seven-dimensional Calabi-Yau space from M-theory. As I had previously surmised, the details of how strings vibrate within this seven-dimensional space were in close agreement with Dogon descriptions and diagrams. (It is worth noting that there are other scientific theories related to string theory, such as torsion theory, that also closely resemble the Dogon cosmological model.)

I now realized that the string theory diagrams constituted direct evidence of science in the Egyptian hieroglyphic language. The name of the mythological Egyptian goddess who was responsible for the creation of matter and the words for the method by which she created it were expressed in the clearest of terms of what could only be described as string theory or some other closely related theory. No well-meaning critic could claim that an anthropologist had misrepresented the resemblance, nor was there much basis for suggesting that it was a coincidence because the hieroglyphs matched not merely one but three separate scientific diagrams. Most important was the context in which the symbols were found—as part of an explicit mythological discussion of the creation of matter. This context had been firmly established by document after document from the beginning to the end of Egyptian culture. The astounding implications behind the meaning of these three ordinary hieroglyphic words were somewhat staggering. They meant that the resemblances between Dogon mythology and science were likely to be far more than wishful thinking. They also implied that the mythologies of the world could actually be speaking truthfully when they state that the skills of civilization were taught to humanity.

As a consequence, I now believe that the floodgates have opened. It is distinctly possible that there is new science to be found in the Egyptian hieroglyphs—those remarkable 5,000-year-old drawings whose mysteries could well provide important clues to modern scientists. Moreover, the very existence of these astonishing symbols among the texts of ancient societies calls for an adjustment in the way that we understand and interpret our own history. These symbols of science also confront us with a host of new and difficult questions, many of which must eventually be answered. The foremost of these might be to ask (this time in all seriousness) who took such great care to help us organize our earliest societies? Who was so very concerned about our eventual development that he or she encoded these essential facts of science into the symbols and stories of our mythologies? We know that many of the most ancient sources considered these teachers to be gods—and surely a person from 3400 BC would have perceived them as such. However, modern Dogon priests insist that they were not gods and specifically say that they referred to themselves simply as "agents of god." Whatever the case may be, there are a few simple observations that can be made about these teachers with some degree of certainty. They knew a lot about science—perhaps more than our scientists know today. Whoever they were, they demonstrated an absolute commitment to helping us. In the end, they went to very great lengths to encode and preserve their message in ways that were carefully calculated to survive and that seemingly were meant to be discovered and recognized. I consider this book a call to the curious and the informed to keep looking for truthful answers to the difficult questions of the world and a challenge to those who are more than able to continue to reach out generously to those who are not yet able.

TWO

THEMES OF THE ANCIENT CREATION STORIES

C reation stories are among the earliest religious artifacts of ancient societies. They presumably evolved first as oral traditions, only later to be put down in written form as emerging civilizations matured. In some cases, as in the Sumerian culture, no explicit written creation story has survived. However, there are many references to the gods of creation and their attributes and actions in nonreligious texts that make it possible to reconstruct an original narrative. The creation tradition of any single culture tended to evolve over time, often with variations from region to region, so scholars are sometimes left with more than one creation story or more than one version of the same story within a given society.

The oldest creation stories center on a surprisingly constant set of themes. If we look at these themes as they appear in the Dogon religion, we find that they can be grouped into two distinct storylines, which I call the surface story line and the deep story line. In the ancient Egyptian and modern Dogon religions, candidates for the priesthood were first introduced to a surface story that established a context for the various religious symbols and concepts, then graduated to a deeper story that defined the inner teachings of the religion. The Dogon tell us that one purpose of this approach was to hold back or disguise the innermost secrets of the religion from all but the most committed candidates.

The surface story line included some or all of the following elements: First, a self-created god emerges from the waters of chaos. The Dogon call this their one true god, Amma. The corresponding Egyptian god is known as Amen, and an equivalent Sumerian goddess called Nammu bears the title of Ama.Tu.An.Ki., meaning "the mother who gave birth to heaven and earth."[1] This self-formed god or goddess then creates a series of godlike entities in pairs, usually eight in number. In the tradition of Heliopolis, these eight were called the Ogdoad, and included Shu and Tefnut, Geb and Nut, Isis and Osiris, and Seth and Nephthys. The members of the four pairs are usually said to be male and female or are cast as opposites, such as darkness and light or day and night. Next, the stars, planets, Earth, and moon are formed. Then, either the self-created god or one of the emergent gods creates the first man and woman, often from clay. In some cultures, the eight paired entities take on the aspect of ancestors of man, like the eight ancestors of the Dogon and the eight Anunnaki of the Sumerians. Many times these same ancestors play the role of educators who teach the skills of civilization to mankind and sometimes serve as founding members of the original families of mankind, ultimately giving birth to eighty offspring (or in some traditions like Islam, forty twin offspring). The most revered or eldest of these ancestors carry a name similar to Leve (as in the Viking myths), Lebe (in the Dogon myths), or Levi (an honored hereditary title in Judaism).

The deep story line typically includes more intimate details than the surface story line about the creation of the formed universe from the unformed universe. Typically, the unformed universe is described as an egg—the Dogon refer to it as Amma's egg—that contains all of the seeds, or signs, of the world. In some cultures these signs are represented as the letters of the alphabet, but in others they are simply identified as the seeds of the world to come. Specific details of the story line vary from culture to culture. For example, in the creation tradition of Hermopolis in Egypt, pairs of serpents and frogs create the egg. In Dogon culture, Amma creates the egg and paired seeds or signs follow. Commonly, an unspecified force causes this cosmic egg to open—the Dogon call it the opening of Amma's eyes—releasing a whirlwind that ultimately forms the spiraling galaxies of stars and planets.

Implied throughout these storylines is a basic set of principles that are exemplified in episodes from the oldest myths of many world cultures and that the Dogon take great care to explicitly define. The first is the principle of twinness, a theme that is apparent in Dogon mythology from the earliest moment of creation. For the Dogon, the universe actually consists of two creations, one that we can see and one that we cannot. In the surface story of the Dogon, the initial act of the self-created god Amma is to form a perfect twin pair, which the Dogon call the Nummo or Nommo. Each of the creative acts that follow occurs in pairs. This same pattern can be seen in the dominant Egyptian creation traditions of Heliopolis and Hermopolis, both of which describe an initial set of emergent godlike entities created in pairs.

A second guiding principle that applies to these sets of twins is the pairing of male and female (e.g., the Japanese male and female deities Izanagi and Izanami). In many societies, we see this principle first expressed in the form of a self-created god who is defined as being androgynous (such as Atum in Egypt or the Hindu god Shiva, who are both male and female), followed by four male and female pairs of emergent gods and goddesses (in the pattern of the Ogdoad of Egypt). Sometimes, this principle is alternately expressed as the pairing of opposites, such as order and chaos (a primordial pairing said to have been created by the Chinese god P'an Ku) or as positive and negative like the Chinese concepts of yin and yang.

These two principles of twinness and the pairing of opposites are evident in virtually all aspects of Dogon culture. For example, it is the Dogon tradition to establish their villages and districts in pairs, which they refer to as upper and lower. We can see this same custom reflected in the traditional organization of ancient Egypt into two lands, one called Upper Egypt and the other called Lower Egypt. Similarly, the two Egyptian lands took colors for their standards—red and white—that are seen as opposites in their culture. These same colors for the Dogon represent success in cattle herding and success in agriculture, respectively. The choice of these symbolic colors—if consonant with the Dogon usage—could suggest a possible deliberate division of labor in early Egypt of the kind that is common in modern Dogon culture, wherein a given plot of land is divided between those who farm and others who forge the tools and implements of farming. The metalworkers receive a share of the crop raised on the plot but are forbidden to actually raise crops themselves.

Beyond these basic guiding principles there are also symbols that are central to the Dogon creation narrative and that turn up again and again in early creation stories from around the world. The first is the image of the spiraling coil, which expresses itself in many different forms and settings and is found as far distant from Egypt as the myths of the Australian aborigines. We see it in images of rams' horns, which occur in nature in two forms—laterally spiraling and coiled. We also see it in images of serpents, creatures that move in a laterally undulating motion and rest in a coil. The serpent symbol is perhaps the single most pervasive and persistent image of the oldest world mythologies. We might also see the theme of spiraling coils in the many ancient references to whirlwinds and storms.

Equal in importance to the spiraling coil is the symbol of water. In the earliest mythologies, the original self-created god is usually said to emerge from the primordial waters or the waters of chaos. Many key gods and goddesses from world mythology—like the Egyptian god Atum, the Nummo of the Dogon, and the ancient Chichimec god Opochtli from Mexico—are specifically said to represent water. In fact, in the Dogon language, the word *nummo* means water. Likewise, the Sumerian god Enki symbolized the waters of the Earth, but his counterpart Enlil represented the air as a kind of fluid that fills the space between the earth and sky.

Another important symbol central to the oldest world mythologies is that of clay, which also appears in many forms. In the Dogon creation story, the planets are like pellets of clay flung out into space at the opening of Amma's egg, and the sun is compared to a clay pot that has been raised to a high heat. In many early mythologies, we are told that the first man and woman were created from clay. Traces of this same creation theme can be seen in the Greek myth of Prometheus, who is said to have molded mankind from clay, and in Japanese myths that state that man was created from clay. Similar primal links to clay and water can be found in the Egyptian religion, as is the case with the Egyptian word *nun*, which was used to express the concept of the primordial waters. The hieroglyphic characters used to write the word *nun* consist of three clay pots and three wavy lines of water, which suggest that the image of the clay pot might also have been an original part of Egyptian creation tradition:

The earliest creation stories place recurring emphasis on the numbers two and eight. For instance, the Dogon say that the Nummo was the perfect twin pair and that the sun is surrounded by a spiral of copper that has eight turns. The original Ogdoad of Egypt consisted of eight gods, just as there were said to be eight original Sumerian Anunnaki.

Numerology is a frequent feature of the earliest religions, such as those in the near eastern cultures of Chaldea and Babylon and in the Vedic tradition of India, and there is a kind of uniformity in the assignment of numbers and meanings among many different cultures. For example, one hallmark of most ancient religions is that the first ten numbers are represented by the first ten letters of the alphabet and that the number ten is considered to be the perfect number (this was true for the Greeks, the Etruscans, and in ancient Judaism). The name for the letter representing ten is often seen as a name for a god. Even today we can see remnants of this kind of symbolic relationship in the Spanish language, in which the word *dios* means God and the word *diez* means ten. Another possible example of this can be found in the very name of Judaism itself, which presumably is taken from the tenth letter of the Hebrew alphabet, *yud*. For the Dogon, other numbers have special numerological significance: three is the number of the male, four is the number of the female, seven is the number of the individual and of the master of language, eight is the number of language itself, and nine is the number of chieftainship. Echoes of this seeming plan of numerology can be found in many other cultures. For instance, in ancient Egyptian art, the number nine can often be found on renderings of the Pharaoh, a custom that is perhaps another expression of the Dogon numerological symbol for chieftainship.

There are obvious similarities in the basic plot and structure of the creation stories of the Dogon, the ancient Egyptians, and the ancient Sumerians. These similarities are reflected in the names, sequences, acts, and configurations of gods and goddesses said to emerge from the waters at the time of creation and are made more obvious when placed side-by-side:

DOGON	EGYPTIAN	SUMERIAN
Amma	Amen/Atum	Ama.Tu.An.Ki/ Nammu
Male & female Nummo	Nehmmu/Khnum	Enki & Enlil
8 ancestors	8 Ogdoad gods plus	8 Anunnaki
8 families/80 members	Horus	40 Anunnaki

The many similarities between the gods of Egypt and those of Meso-potamia were noticed by Sir E. A. Wallis Budge, author of the hiero-glyphic dictionary. In *The Gods of the Egyptians,* he sought underlying reasons to explain the perplexing issue of these similarities:

It is surprising therefore to find so much similarity existing between the primeval gods of Sumer and those of Egypt, especially as the resemblance cannot be the result of borrowing. It is out of the ques-tion to assume that Ashur-banipal's editors borrowed the system from Egypt, or that the literary men of the time of Seti I borrowed their ideas from the *literati* of Babylonia or Assyria, and we are therefore driven to the conclusion that both the Sumerians and the early Egyptians derived their primeval gods from some common but exceedingly ancient source. The similarity between the two companies of gods seems to be too close to be accidental.[2]

Similarly, respected members of the modern academic community such as French historian Nicholas Grimal are also quite aware of the correlations that exist between the ancient Egyptian religion and modern Dogon mythology. Grimal commented on some of these similarities in his book *A History of Ancient Egypt:*

Anubis recalls the incestuous jackal in a Promethean role which existed prior to the Nummos among the Dogon people of Mali, whose cosmology also depends on eight original gods. There are further African links with Egypt: Amun, for instance, resembles the golden heavenly ram whose brow is adorned with horns and a gourd reminiscent of the solar disc; Osiris recalls Lebe, whose resurrection is announced by the regrowth of the millet; and finally, each individual was thought to be made up of a soul and a vital essence . . . which the Egyptians called the *ba* and the *ka*.[3]

In many of the earliest religions of the world, the first three emergent gods and goddesses are said to represent—in one form or another—Water, Air, and Earth. However, the symbolism attached to these entities can often be somewhat complicated. Typically the goddess of the Air is said to represent humidity, the atmosphere, or air conceived as a fluid. The god of the Earth often represents, in some complex way, the waters of the Earth. For reasons that have not been fully explained, there is a persistent intrusion of water into the symbolism of these earliest gods and goddesses that serves to complicate our understanding of their roles. The first self-created god and goddess might be typified by a kind of vagueness of description, often with few specific attributes or qualities assigned to them. Generally, the female member of the first twin pair of entities is associated with air, the atmosphere, storms, and the arts of weaving and language. The male member is more often symbolized by a ram, goat, or other horned animal and associated with the arts of pottery and metalworking. Thus in the Egyptian religion we have Khnum, the ram-headed god who created animals, and the god Ptah, who created heaven and earth and was identified with the Greek god Hephaistos, the mythological blacksmith.

Along with these emergent gods and goddesses whose lineage is clearly stated, we find another type of goddess whose relationship to the stories of creation is less clearly defined. Many of the earliest cultures honor an original mother goddess, often said to be the oldest deity and to have given birth to all of the other gods. The Dogon creation story makes no obvious reference to a separate goddess in this role (although the Dogon word *dada*—also the name of the spider who weaves matter —means "mother"), but the Sumerians assign this place to Nammu, the goddess whose title was Ama.Tu.An.Ki. This title shows possible roots with the names of the Dogon god Amma and the Sumerian god Enki (An. Ki), just as there is a suggestive relationship between the Dogon Nummo and the Sumerian Nammu. Egyptian mythology also identifies an original mother goddess, Net (popularly known as Neith). One of the earliest Egyptian temples was founded by the first king of Egypt and dedicated to the goddess Neith—perhaps originally a Libyan goddess—who was said to be the mother of the numberless Egyptian gods.

Another concept of great importance to the earliest religions is the idea of the cardinal points of the Earth—north, south, east, and west. Many of the earliest religious symbols included features that were meant to represent these four points. This can be seen in the four corners of the Jewish *tallis*, which are brought together in one hand to symbolize the unity of God. This is done during the morning prayer service, just before the recitation of the Shema—the central prayer of Judaism. It is a well-known fact that important structures of the ancient world, like the Great Pyramid of Egypt, were carefully and deliberately aligned with the four cardinal points. (Many others were aligned with individual stars.) This follows in the tradition of the *stupa*, or *chorten*, an ancient form of aligned shrine commonly found across India and Asia. In some early mythologies, such as those of some Native American tribes like the

Navaho, the sky was said to be supported by four great posts or pillars, each of which was identified with one of the four cardinal points.

Another concept that is carefully defined by the Dogon religion and persistently found among other early religions is that of the "Word." The Dogon use this term literally to refer to actual speech and language, but they also use it figuratively to mean the acquisition of a skill or knowledge of a concept. For example, in Dogon mythology the concept of clothing as exemplified by the first fiber skirt is said to represent the First Word, and mastery of the skill of weaving constitutes the Second Word. In these examples, the concept of the Word can be taken figuratively to mean instruction in civilizing skills—in essence, words in the language of civilization. A related concept in Dogon mythology is the notion of words being woven into the cloth. This concept is introduced with the statement that the vapor from the Nummos' breath as they spoke was absorbed into the strands of the first fiber skirt. Together these two Dogon concepts, if truly derived from the same symbolic system as that of ancient Egypt, can be seen as the likely precursors of later Christian symbolism, which refers to the Word of God and to priests as men of the cloth.

Because these themes, symbols, and concepts reappear so frequently in the earliest mythologies, their prominence makes them pivotal to any comparative understanding of those mythologies. Likewise, the creation myths of the Dogon assume an important role in this process of understanding because of their unique ability to explain these symbols and concepts in plain and understandable terms.

THREE

THE DOGON
CREATION STORY

Before we can begin to make detailed comparisons based on the symbols found in the Dogon cosmological myths, we must first familiarize ourselves with the surface story line of the Dogon creation story. Although the Dogon have a sophisticated spoken language and an extensive catalog of religious symbols and signs, they do not possess a written language, so there has been no indigenous written version of the Dogon creation story. Because of this, Marcel Griaule and Germaine Dieterlen found themselves faced with the formidable task of constructing a written story from various Dogon oral myths and drawings and from the knowledge and insight of a group of elder Dogon priests. Dogon cosmology is actually shared with a small group of related tribes who live in close proximity to the Dogon (including the Arou, the Bozo, and the Bambara), so the final written version came to include contributions from elders of each of the related tribes. Part of the challenge for the anthropologists was to reconcile differences between various versions of the myths to produce what constitutes a consensus of Dogon thought and belief. When appropriate, Griaule and Dieterlen included alternate versions of the same myth in their finished text to accurately reflect differences in Dogon schools of thought. It is important to remember that, in the surface story line, some of the original Dogon concepts were intentionally simplified and others made more complex as a way of disguising references to the deepest secrets of the religion.

No doubt the surface narrative of the Dogon creation story is best expressed in Griaule's book *Conversations with Ogotemmeli,* a short work that reflects his understanding of the Dogon myths based on several years of on-site observation and thirty-three days of specific instruction by the Dogon priest. *The Pale Fox* is Griaule and Dieterlen's finished anthropological study of the Dogon religion, and it includes a more intimate discussion of Dogon symbols and concepts, taken from what I call the "deep story line." Because the current study draws primarily from the works of Griaule and Dieterlen for information about the Dogon, the following summary of the surface creation story of the Dogon has been paraphrased from Griaule's work in *Conversations with Ogotemmeli.*

———

The Dogon say that the stars were created from pellets of earth flung out into space by the one true god, Amma. The sun and the moon were created by a process much like that of making pottery, which was the first known invention of god. The sun is like a pot that has been fired until it is white-hot, then surrounded by a spiral of copper with eight turns. To create the Earth, Amma squeezed a lump of clay in his hand and threw it away from himself in the same manner as he did the stars. The clay spread to the north and to the south (the top and the bottom) in a movement that was horizontal. By nature, the Earth is female. Looking at it flat and considering the cardinal points of the compass as her appendages, it is like a woman lying on her back with her arms and legs spread. The anthill is her female organ. In the course of time, Amma tried to fertilize her, but in what was a breach of order in the universe, proper intercourse could not take place. In the universe, there is a principle of twin births, but this flawed union between god and Earth created only one being, the jackal, which became the symbol of disorder and the difficulties of god. Later, having overcome the difficulty, god had intercourse with the Earth again, this time successfully. Water, which is the divine seed, entered the womb of the Earth and resulted in the birth of twins. Two beings were formed, which god created like water. They were green in color and were half human, half serpent. Their bodies were green and sleek all over and shiny like the surface of the water. These spirits were called Nummo, and they were born perfect. They had eight members, and their number was eight, which is also the symbol of speech. They were of divine essence, which is the life force of the world, and is water. The name Nummo is synonymous in the Dogon language with the word for water. To the Dogon, Nummo is water, and the Nummo pair is present in all water—whether it is drinking water, water of the river, or water of storms.

In *Conversations with Ogotemmeli*, Griaule included Ogotemmeli's description of this relationship:

> The life-force of the earth is water. God moulded the earth with water. Blood too he made out of water. Even in a stone there is this force, for there is moisture in everything. But if Nummo is water, it also produces copper. When the sky is overcast, the sun's rays may be seen materializing on the misty horizon. These rays, excreted by the spirits, are of copper and are light. They are water too, because they uphold the earth's moisture as it rises. The Pair excrete light, because they are also light.[1]

After the defilement of the Earth during the first ill-fated attempt at intercourse, god decided to create man directly. He formed a womb and a male organ from two lumps of clay. These lumps developed into the first pair of humans, a male and a female. Man, who is usually born one at a time, violated the mythological principle of twin births, so to atone for this, man was given two souls, one male and one female.

The first man and woman had intercourse with each other and gave birth in pairs to a series of eight children, who became the eight ancestors. The first four were male, the next four female. In the beginning, the eight ancestors did not know death but lived on indefinitely. By a *special dispensation permitted only to them, they were able to fertilize themselves.*

The Nummo twins represent the ideal unit. When the Nummo looked down at the Earth and saw it unclothed and speechless, they decided to put an end to the disorder and confusion. The Nummo came down to Earth, bringing with them the fibers of plants created in heaven. From these fibers they created the first garment, which was made of two strands of ten fibers—one strand worn in front, the other in back. The way the fibers hung in spiraling coils was symbolic of the water of tornadoes and hurricanes. The fibers themselves were reminiscent of the sun, which dries up moisture, and were also like the speech of the Nummo, which comes out in a warm vapor of water, the sound of which tapers off in spiraling coils. In this sense, the moisture of the words of the Nummo was transferred to the fibers of the garment. This fiber skirt was called the First Word.

In the anthill, the male Nummo assumed the role of the masculine element, and the female Nummo took the role of the female element. After a time, instinct led the oldest of the eight ancestors toward the anthill, wearing a wooden bowl on his head to protect him from rain. He put his feet into the opening of the anthill and sank in, all except the bowl, which became caught on the edges of the opening. This freed him from his role as a physical being, and he was taken under the guidance of the Nummo pair. He followed the male Nummo into the depths of the Earth, where, in the waters of the Earth's womb, he curled up like a fetus, shrank to germinal form, and acquired the quality of water, the seed of god, and the essence of the two Nummo spirits. Just as the eight copper spirals give the sun its movement, the spiral of the Word gave the womb its regenerative movement. All eight ancestors, one by one, had to be transformed in this way.

Now, three is the number of the male element. Four is the number of the female element. The seventh object or event in a series represents completion, even though it is not inherently better than any of the others, because it is the sum of the male and female elements.

The words that the female Nummo spoke to herself turned into a spiral and entered into her sexual part, and the male Nummo helped her. These words are what the seventh ancestor learned while inside the womb. The seventh ancestor received perfect knowledge of the Second Word, which was not reserved for particular recipients but was meant for all mankind. During his transformation, the seventh ancestor developed slowly in the womb of the Earth. On the day when his transformation was complete, he emerged at sunrise and, using his teeth as weaver's reeds and the movement of his jaws to create a shuttle action, invented the art of weaving. While weaving, he imparted technical instruction so that people could understand the process, demonstrating by example the need for harmony between spiritual forces and physical actions. The words that the spirit spoke were woven into the cloth as it was created— they were the cloth, which was the Word.

The Dogon call woven material *soy*, which means, "It is the spoken word." Soy also means seven, after the seventh ancestor.

The Nummo, acting on behalf of Amma, planned to initiate projects to improve and redeem mankind, but they were concerned about the effect of contact between spiritual beings such as themselves and people of flesh and blood. So after their transformations, the eight ancestors were taken to heaven with the Nummo to learn the skills of civilization. Later, each was given one of the eight grains of heaven, and they returned to live with men again, bringing with them their newly learned skills.

Until that time, people had lived in holes dug in the soil. Then they noticed the shape of the anthill, which they found to be much better than their earthen holes. They copied its shape and made mud huts, added rooms and passageways, and began to use them to store food.

This improved anthill was the precursor of the granary, which would be introduced as the next divine concept and constituted the Third Word.

When the first ancestor came down from heaven, he was standing on a square piece of heaven shaped like the first granary.

The first granary was shaped like a woven basket turned upside down. It was round at the bottom, square and flat at the top (with an inscribed circle), and wider at the bottom than the top. There were stairways with ten steps up the middle of each of the four sides, which faced toward the cardinal points of north, south, east, and west. The door of the granary was at the sixth step of the north side. Inside were two levels containing eight chambers each. The structural features of the granary had symbolic meaning:

The round base represented the sun. The square roof represented the sky. A circle in the center of the roof represented the moon. The rise of each step was male; the tread was female. The combined total of forty steps (eighty males and females) represented the eighty offspring of the eight ancestors.

Each stairway was associated with a constellation or planet and a group of creatures. The northern stairway was associated with the Pleiades and represented men and fish. The southern one was associated with the belt of Orion and represented domesticated animals. The eastern one was associated with Venus and represented birds, and the western one was associated with what the Dogon called the long-tailed star and represented wild animals, vegetables, and insects. The ten steps up each side of the granary represented different family orders of the animal and plant kingdoms.

For the Dogon, there is also symbolism associated with the eight compartments of the granary, four of which were on the lower level and four on the upper. The compartments were separated by two intersecting partitions, which met at a cup-shaped depression in the earth large enough to hold a round jar. The jar, which held grain or objects of value, was the center of the whole building. The compartments were numbered from one to eight, moving counterclockwise around the lower level starting with the front/right compartment, then continuing on the upper level, again starting with the front/right compartment. The granary, like the Earth in earlier descriptions, represented a woman lying on her back with her arms and legs spread—the jar was her womb, the four uprights that supported corners of the roof were her arms and legs. Her legs were on the north side, and the door represented her sexual parts. The woman also represented the sun, and her arms and legs, which supported the roof, represented the sky.

In another way, the granary also represented the internal organs of the body and showed the circulation of nourishment within a body. Nourishment flowed from the first two compartments, which represented the stomach and gizzard, then moved symbolically into the intestines (compartment six) and into all of the other compartments as symbolic blood and breath. From there it moved into the final compartments, which represented the liver and gall bladder. The Dogon consider breath to be vapor, a form of water, which is the sustaining principle of life.

Assembled on the flat roof of the granary were the tools of a forge, which were to be used by the first ancestor to teach man to make iron tools for cultivating the land. The bellows were made out of two twin clay pots connected by a sheepskin. The shape of the two pots represented the sun. The sheepskin was a symbol of the celestial ram, which was the avatar, or animal representation, of the male Nummo. The hammer was an iron block with a handle shaped like a cone. The anvil was fixed in a beam of wood. The smith ancestor had an iron bow and spindles for arrows. He shot one arrow into the center of the circle on the roof of the granary, which represented the moon, and he wrapped a long thread around the shank to form a bobbin. He shot a second arrow into the air, which attached to the vault of the sky.

Together with the granary, this created an entire system of symbols:

The granary represented the new system of the world. It defined a unit of volume. The height of each step was a unit of length, the cubit. The flat, square roof was eight cubits long on each side. The square roof and the round base were examples of the two primary geometric figures. Symbolically, the granary represented the shape of an iron shuttle used for ginning cotton. It also represented the head of the hammer, which is male, and the four-sided anvil, which is female. Additionally, it was an image of the webbed hands of the Nummo, of which the hammer was also an image. Finally, it represented the female body, which is the female element of the smith, who like all beings, was dual in nature. To create the original fire of the smithy, the ancestor stole embers, which were a piece of the sun, from the workshop of the Nummo, who are heaven's smiths. To steal the embers, he used a "robber's stick," the crook of which opened in a slit that was like an open mouth. On the way back to the granary's smithy, the ancestor accidentally dropped some embers and had to come back to pick them up. He then fled toward the granary but, in the anxiety of his escape, could not locate its entrance. He went around it several times before he found the steps and climbed up to the flat roof, where he hid the embers in the skin of the bellows. He exclaimed "Gouyo!" which meant "stolen."

Today in the Dogon language, *gouyo* means "granary." It is a reminder that there would be no grain to store without the fire of the smithy, from which iron hoes are made.

The art of pottery came to be associated with the smithy:

The wife of the smith had made a pot, shaped like the clay pots of the bellows, which she was letting dry in the sun. Hoping it would dry more quickly, she moved it closer to the fire of the smithy and found that the heat made the pot harden. From that day on, she was in the habit of firing her pots. Pottery was originally the exclusive domain of the wives of the smiths, but later it became permissible for any woman to practice pottery.

At this point, the ancestor was ready to begin the work of establishing civilization, starting with the teaching of agriculture. He came down the northern stairway and measured out a square field, eighty cubits on each side, oriented to the cardinal points of north, south, east, and west, just like the granary. The field was divided into eighty-by-eighty units, each one square cubit, which were distributed among the families of the eight ancestors. Mud houses for the families were built along the centerline of the land, which ran from north to south. The smithy was established to the north of this line.

The Dogon believed that the earth had been pure when it was originally created but that the jackal's birth made it impure and had disrupted the world order. Agriculture was a symbol for the restoration of order to the pure earth, and wherever agriculture and civilization spread, the impurity of the earth was thought to have receded.

According to Ogotemmeli, the original method of cultivation was like weaving; it began on the north side and moved from east to west, then back again. Each square in the field contained eight planted rows, each eight feet long, in memory of the eight ancestors and the eight seeds. The Dogon say that when a man clears new ground, makes a plot, and plants food on the plot, his work is like weaving a cloth. In this way, the skill of agriculture is a form of weaving.

Although all eight families were of equal rank, the eighth had a special privilege. Seven is the number of the master of speech, whose job it was to teach speech, but eight is the number of speech itself. Because the oldest living Dogon man belonged to the eighth family, he of all living beings most truly represented the Word. His name was Lebe.

When the first ancestor, who was the smith, had finished his instruction, the seven other ancestors descended to teach their skills of civilization to man. These skills included leatherworking, music, and so on, and were taught in order of rank. However, the eighth ancestor took his place out of turn and came down before the seventh, who was the master of speech. This made the seventh ancestor so very angry that he turned against the others, took the form of a great serpent, and tried to remove the heavenly grains from the granary. The smith saw the serpent as an adversary and in order to rid himself of it, advised men to kill the snake.

Ogotemmeli considered this dispute a turning point in the history of the world.

FOUR

DOGON SYMBOLS
AND MEANINGS

The surface narrative of the Dogon creation story presents themes and incidents that should seem quite familiar to students of ancient mythologies. The sequence and manner in which the godlike entities of the Dogon religion emerge is comparable to that of the earliest Egyptian, Sumerian, and Akkadian religious traditions. The creation story itself includes subplots, such as the incident in which the Dogon ancestor steals the fire of the Nummo, that we find repeated later in the fables of Greek mythology. Likewise, there are many obvious resemblances between Dogon symbolism and that of Mayan mythology. For example, both cultures conceive of the Earth as a woman lying on her back, her arms and legs representing the cardinal compass points. The roughly pyramidal shape and dimensions of the Dogon granary call to mind the early mastabas of ancient Egypt, and we find many of the symbolic aspects of the Dogon granary repeated in the flat-topped pyramids of the Americas. The more familiar we become with the deep symbolism of the Dogon creation story, the more we will see that these similarities extend to some of the most remote corners of the world and resonate with the mythologies of societies as diverse as those of the Maori of New Zealand, the earliest cultures of Asia, and even the native tribes of North America.

If it is our goal to understand more about the meaning of Dogon religious symbols, then the most obvious place to start is with observations of the anthropologists who most closely studied them. Although Griaule and Dieterlen did not venture to interpret possible meanings for individual Dogon symbols beyond what the Dogon themselves stated, it was their opinion that the Dogon religious system should be seen as much more than a simple tribal mythology. In their view, it represents a serious and careful discussion of the fundamental forces at work in the physical world. This opinion is openly and unambiguously stated in the various writings of Griaule and Dieterlen:

> Having observed and studied everything within range of their perception, they have constructed an indigenous explanation of the manifestations of nature (anthropology, botany, zoology, geology, astronomy, anatomy, and physiology) as well as social facts (social structures, religious and political structures, crafts, arts, economy, etc.). The Dogon possess a system of signs or ideographs including several thousands, an astronomy and calendars, a numerical system, extensive physiological and anatomical knowledge, genetics, and a systematic pharmacopoeia. . . . The world is conceived as a whole, this whole having been thought, realized, and organized by one creator God in a complete system which includes disorder. . . . The development of Dogon thought, and hence the elaboration of concepts, proceeds by analogy and has constant recourse to the symbol. . . . Thus, the symbol plays the role "of conveyor of knowledge." . . . The value and efficacy of the symbol are such in this system, that the Dogon declare that it is not the thing itself, but "the symbol alone which is essential." . . . In the religious domain, this system is linked together by the existence of elaborate myths dealing with the fundamental notion of God, the history of the creation of the world, of the establishment of order and the appearance of disorder. . . . The myth [which the Dogon call] so tanie "astonishing word" which the Dogon consider to be "real" history . . . constitutes here the whole of coherent themes of creation; this is why, by virtue of their coherence and their order of succession, they make up a "history of the universe," aduno so tanie.[1]

Any notion that the Dogon myths should be seen as representations of simple folklore is explicitly rejected by Griaule and Dieterlen.

> By no means . . . should the word of the myth be understood in its ordinary sense, as a childlike or fantastic, somewhat absurd poetic form. The myth is . . . only a means by which to explain something; it is a consciously composed lore of master ideas which may not be placed within reach of just anyone at any time. . . . It conceals clear statements and coherent systems reserved for initiates, who alone have access to the "deep knowledge." The myths present themselves in layers, like the shells of a seed, and one of their reasons for being is precisely to cover and conceal from the profane a precious seed which appears to belong rightly to a universal, valid body of knowledge.[2]

Also rejected by Griaule and Dieterlen is a view that the Dogon myths should be interpreted as simple adventure tales, perhaps comparable to the heroic Greek myths:

> The Dogon myth does not relate facts merely involving adventures, rivalries between the gods, or the effects of love and hate . . . such as they are presented by other religions. . . . Rather it shows evidence of serious examination of the very conditions of life and death; hence, its precise biological aspect. . . . The myth presents a construction of the universe—from that of the stellar system down to that of the smallest grain.[3]

> Among the Dogon exoteric myths correspond to a "superficial knowledge" common to the greater part of the population; on the other hand, esoteric myths, parallel to these, present other identifications and much wider connexions. Finally, within and beyond this totality of beliefs appears a logical scheme of symbols expressing a system of thought which cannot be described simply as myth. For this conceptual structure, when studied, reveals an internal

coherence, a secret wisdom, and an apprehension of ultimate realities equal to that which we Europeans conceive ourselves to have attained.[4]

Another useful reference when it comes to understanding Dogon words and phrases is the *Dictionnaire Dogon,* compiled by Genevieve Calame-Griaule, daughter of Marcel Griaule and a respected anthropologist in her own right. The dictionary confirms Marcel Griaule's translation of *aduno* as "universe" and *so tanie* as "astonishing word." However, a close examination shows that the word *aduno* can also mean "symbols," the word *so* can mean "to speak," and the word *ta* means "to do something discreetly or in a way that does not transgress." So, an alternate meaning for the phrase *aduno so tanie* might well be "symbols that are spoken about discreetly." A loose but more concise translation might be "secret symbols" or "hidden symbols."

Griaule, Dieterlen, and Calame-Griaule lend strong encouragement to those who would seek concrete meaning in the symbols of Dogon mythology. There is no doubt that any search for deeper meaning in the surface narrative of the creation story should focus first on the major themes of the myths because it is to these ideas and concepts that the story line repeatedly draws our attention. Among these themes, the first that comes to mind is that of water because previous discussion has shown water to be the central image in each ancient mythology. It might seem more than coincidental that every member of each triad of gods discussed previously is defined first in terms of water, most of the Dogon and Egyptian symbols relating to creation refer back to water, and many of the Egyptian hieroglyphs pertaining to the concepts of creation are expressed using the symbols of water. So, an obvious first step in an effort to assign meanings to the symbols would be to reconsider what we know about water, starting with Griaule's statement from Ogotemmeli about the meaning of water:

The life-force of the earth is water. God moulded the earth with water. Blood too he made out of water. Even in a stone there is this force, for there is moisture in everything. . . . When the sky is overcast, the sun's rays may be seen materializing on the misty horizon. These rays . . . are water, too, because they uphold the earth's moisture as it rises.[5]

The Dogon understanding of the nature of water as expressed by Ogotemmeli corresponds remarkably well to descriptions of water as they appear in any encyclopedia or reference book. Such articles—like the *Encyclopedia Britannica* entry for water—reaffirm that living matter is primarily composed of water, that the major component of life-giving fluids in plants and animals is water, that water settles in rock beds beneath the earth and within rocks themselves, and that water vapor rises due to the heat of the sun, only to fall back to Earth again as precipitation. The content of Ogotemmeli's description and that from an encyclopedia, taken side by side, are strikingly and thoroughly similar—so completely similar that the Dogon rendition could almost be inserted in the reference book and not significantly alter the meaning. In fact, a student could learn nearly as much from Ogotemmeli's statements about water as from a modern encyclopedia. This similarity lends support to Griaule and Dieterlen's assessment of the Dogon creation story as a serious presentation of fact and provides us with a possible clue about the kind of information to be looked for in the myths. It suggests that what lies behind the symbols of a story is a kind of basic encyclopedic information—general, factual knowledge, organized and presented so as to inform.

A random survey of encyclopedia articles about water shows that most are organized in a similar and predictable way. First they present information about the molecular structure of water (H_2O), then tell about the three physical states of water (liquid, solid, and vapor), then discuss the natural water cycle, explaining how water is evaporated to form clouds, which then cause precipitation, which falls to earth and collects in streams, rivers, and groundwater, and eventually makes its way back to the sea to be evaporated and form clouds again. If Ogotemmeli's statements about water and those from an encyclopedia article are just coincidentally similar, then we would not expect the creation myths to include useful information about the molecular structure or physical states of water, nor would we expect to find discussion about the natural water cycle.

However, when we reexamine the Dogon creation myth from this perspective and look specifically for information about water, what we find is somewhat surprising. The numbers two and eight are the numbers of the electron structure of water. Hydrogen provides the first two electrons as a twin pair of atoms, and oxygen supplies the additional eight electrons. If we suppose for a moment based on this fact that the Nummo pair represents hydrogen, then what the Dogon say is quite true, that the Nummo pair is found in all water, whether it be water we drink, water of a river, or the water of storms. This information should not surprise us because the Dogon tell us again and again in the most explicit ways that Nummo is water. Likewise, the rays of the sun could reasonably be seen as the excrement of the Nummo because we know that solar energy is a by-product of the fusion of hydrogen atoms, which are in this sense the Nummo pair. So, by simply assuming what the story plainly tells us to be true, that Nummo means water, we are able to explain what Griaule was not able to ascertain from Ogotemmeli's explanation, how a symbol that represents water could also represent the "burning rays of the sun."[6]

The Dogon also express their enigmatic belief that "there is water in copper." If we take a hint from the creation story's use of the water symbol and look at the atomic structure of copper, we might also make sense of this statement. Like many atoms, the electron structure of copper contains two electrons in the innermost electron ring and eight electrons in the second ring—a repetition of the number symbols found in water. So—odd as it may seem that members of an outwardly primitive tribal culture could know this—structurally copper "has water in it," just as the Dogon said. Our success in using this same approach to explain the Dogon statement about copper helps to verify that we are on the right track in our understanding of the symbol of water. The inclusion within the creation story of two such similar statements relating to atomic structure confirms both interpretations as intended meanings.

From our earlier discussion about the Sumerian gods An, Enlil, and Enki, we may recall the difficulties that scholars have faced when trying to categorize these three deities simply as gods of the heavens, the earth, and the waters, respectively, and the persistent link to water that comes into play in their symbolism. We may also recall differences in the symbolism of equivalent deities from culture to culture, as in the case of Enlil, Bel, and Neith, who are in some instances identified as gods or goddesses of the air (conceived of as a liquid), in others as gods of the atmosphere, and in still others as gods of vapor or humidity. However, if we step back and take a broader look at the complete triad of gods in any one culture, we quickly realize that as a group they might more aptly be represented as the three states of water—liquid, solid, and vapor. Our encyclopedias tell us that water is the only substance that naturally occurs in all three of these states at temperatures of normal, daily life. Since ice is not a substance that would be familiar to the experience of a society living in a subtropical area of the world (in fact, Budge includes no entries in his *Hieroglyphic Dictionary* for the words "ice," "freeze," or "frozen"), the images of hardened clay and moisture in rocks might have been substituted for ice as the solid form of water. When we test this supposition by applying the meaning of the word "clay" to Enki, Ea, and Khnum, we find that it draws together the divergent images of a god of dryness, a god of the earth, and a god of the waters of the earth in a way that makes complete sense. In a similar way, the assignment of water vapor as the symbol of our goddesses of the air helps us integrate the symbols of various gods and goddess who are alternately represented by the atmosphere, moisture, and humidity.

Continuing along this same path and using our encyclopedia articles on water as a guide, we would next expect to find somewhere in the creation myths a discussion of the natural water cycle of the earth. In fact, in *Conversations with Ogotemmeli*, Griaule discusses the Dogon understanding of the celestial ram as a symbol for the natural water cycle. To briefly summarize the symbols as the Dogon know them, the calabash between the horns of the ram represents the sun, the horns themselves collect the waters of the rain, the fleece of the ram symbolizes the ground that soaks up the water, and his urine is symbolic of precipitation. When the ram moves among the high clouds, his hooves leave a trail of four colors—black, red, green, and yellow—that for the Dogon are the colors of the rainbow. As we mentioned earlier, Griaule quoted Ogotemmeli as saying, "To draw up and then return what one had drawn—that is the life of the world." The presence of the symbols anticipated by our supposition in the Dogon creation story and each in conjunction with expected meanings of water shows a degree of intention behind the organization of the myths that goes beyond coincidence.

Now, if we return to the original creation story and insert these water-related meanings in place of the corresponding Dogon symbols, the first portion of the myth can be read as a sensible statement about the creation of the universe. In it, the stars are said to be pellets of clay flung into space by Amma at the opening of an egg, which is the familiar scenario of the big bang theory of modern science. (James Bennett Pritchard mentions as a note regarding the Egyptian story of the creation of the universe by Atum that "the creation of Shu . . . and of Tefnut was as explosive as a sneeze."[7]) The art of pottery therefore is established as a metaphor for the act of creating. The stars—Amma's clay pellets—represent the original matter of the universe that science tells us coalesced under the influence of gravity to form stars and planets. In this context, the Dogon are correct that the sun is like a pot raised to a high heat—a body of matter massive enough to attain fusion—and surrounded by a copper coil with eight turns. Here copper might be used as a metaphor for sunlight (based on its color) to introduce the image of spiraling coils and imply the rotation of the sun. In fact, modern science actually defines eight separate zones or spheres that make up the sun—the core, the radiant zone, the convection zone, the photosphere, the sunspots, the magnetic field, the corona, and the solar wind. According to Griaule, the Dogon know that the sun is "in some sort a star," a belief that is also in complete agreement with science. Amma created the Nummo, the perfect twin pair that represents hydrogen, the very element that science tells us was most abundant in the primordial universe, along with lesser amounts of oxygen and carbon. The sun's rays, which we know are the by-product of the fusion of hydrogen atoms, are said to be the excrement of the Nummo. Again, this is in complete agreement with modern science. The Nummo pair with eight members represents water, which the Dogon say is the essence of life, and again science agrees. The Dogon are absolutely correct when they say that the Nummo pair is found in all water and tell us explicitly that Nummo is water, just as the Egyptians clearly tell us that Nun and Atum are water.

The Dogon creation story also relates information about the earth. The Dogon believe that the initial creation of the earth was flawed because the world did not contain water. This statement from mythology is supported by many present-day astronomers who feel that the earth at the time of formation did not contain the necessary water to support life. They theorize that the bulk of earth's water was delivered here by comets. This process, just as the Dogon describe it, is akin to an act of fertilization because without water there could be no life on earth. We find a clear presentation of this theory in a 1999 edition of *Science News*:

> The origin of terrestrial water has perplexed scientists for decades. Astronomers have proposed that comets, the frozen, water-bearing émigrés from the outer solar system, could have delivered much of the Earth's water during the first few hundred million years of the planet's existence. During this epoch, known as the late heavy bombardment, comets pelted the Earth and the other inner planets at a far higher rate than they do today.[8]

There are also emerging theories about another process, very much like the Dogon story of Amma's fertilization of the earth, that describe the delivery of organic molecules to the earth by meteor. A summary of the process was presented in the March 25, 2000, edition of *Science News*:

> A new study shows that carbon molecules known as fullerenes can originate outside the solar system and ride in on meteors. Fullerenes

are hollow, spherical molecules made of pure carbon. . . . This research lends support to the idea that organic molecules from space could have played a role in starting the chemical processes necessary for the origin of life.[9]

It can be seen from the preceding exercise that if we replace the symbols of the Dogon creation story with basic attributes of water gleaned from encyclopedias, the result is a statement about the creation of the universe and the creation of the earth that is organized, succinct, and factually correct. Not only are the facts presented just the ones we would expect to find in an encyclopedia article on water, they also appear in the same logical and organized sequence. More importantly, the interpretation that brings us to this conclusion begins by substituting facts about water for a symbol that we are emphatically told means water and ends by validating both the obvious and the enigmatic statements of the Dogon. We could hardly ask for better proof of a supposition.

The other obvious themes of the Dogon creation story relate to fertilization and the creation of life. Images of intercourse and fertilization appear again and again throughout the myths of each of the civilizations we have discussed—those from Egypt, Sumer, Babylon, Rome, Greece, Central America, Mali, and others as far distant as New Zealand. Symbol after symbol is said to represent a woman, her reproductive parts, the divine seed, and so forth. If we review the Dogon creation story again taking the same analytical approach as before but this time applying meanings that relate to fertilization and the creation of life to the symbols, we find that we are rewarded with similarly satisfying results. In this case, Amma represents the first living single cell, which, according to modern science, emerged self-created from the waters of the ancient ocean, described by scientists as a kind of primordial soup. The perfect Nummo pair is then formed by mitosis, a form of cell division. This process of splitting results in a matching pair of new cells, each with the same chromosomal makeup as the original cell.

The eight ancestors of the Dogon, much like the first eight emergent Egyptian gods and goddesses, could then be seen as an example of the more complicated sexual reproductive process called meiosis. During sexual reproduction, a male and a female organism each contribute a germ cell containing only half of the usual number of chromosomes. Two cells—one from each organism—must divide in a way that is unique to the process of meiosis to form germ cells. The result is four germ cells— two from the male and two from the female.

The surface narrative of the Dogon myth tells about the creation of the eight ancestors, the first four of whom are male, the last four female. Looking at this aspect of the story for a moment as a description of the differentiation of germ cells during the process of meiosis, we can see that the formation of the four male and four female ancestors is in accordance with the description of cell division during the process of meiosis. Since the creation of germ cells in this manner applies only to the process of meiosis, we can now make sense of the Dogon statement that the eight ancestors were allowed to "self-fertilize" by a "special dispensation" granted only to them. We can also understand the statement that the "eight ancestors did not know death" if we consider the relative longevity of the female egg cell, which in comparison with other cells of the body is essentially immortal and also consider the passing on of genetic information to later generations, which might be seen as a form of true immortality.

The next section of the Dogon creation story can easily be seen as a description of sexual reproduction—in fact, it can hardly be seen as anything else. It has already been established that the form of a women can represent the Earth, and we have been told that an anthill represents her sexual organ. The story tells that the eighth ancestor, who symbolizes one of eight germ cells, descends into the opening of the earth and disappears, but he leaves behind the hard wooden bowl he wears on his head because it catches on the sides of the opening. This is almost a clinical description of a sperm as it enters an egg at the moment of fertilization, an act that causes the egg to become impenetrable to other sperm. The description of the Nummo as half man and half serpent, or as having the head of a fish over the head of a man with the tail of a serpent, is the very image of a sperm cell and might well be what is pictured in the

Egyptian symbol of the Eye of Ra 👁. The very odd story of weaving being introduced by the first transformed ancestor, which involves the interweaving of thin fibers between the teeth of the ancestor, might describe the interweaving of the thin chromosome filaments within the fertilized egg to create a complete new set of DNA. An interesting detail relating to reproduction can be found in the Egyptian creation myth of Hermopolis, in which the eight ancestors are represented by pairs of serpents and frogs that form an egg—in scientific terms, a zygote. This detail is echoed by the Dogon concept of the egg of Amma, in which, according to the deep story line for the Dogon, the original creation was supposed to have occurred. It seems more than appropriate and fitting in what appears to be an allegory about sexual reproduction that germ cells would represent the ancestors.

Another Dogon story, about the ancestor who fires an arrow into the vault of the sky and forms a spindle, is a likely reference to the growth process that continues after the sperm and egg join. During this process, a spindle or scaffold is formed, along which the chromosomes move as they separate in two halves at opposite ends of the cell, in preparation for the cell to divide.

The Dogon describe the journey of the eighth ancestor into the anthill as entering the womb of the earth, and it is a journey that each of the eight ancestors must take in turn during the process of transformation, just as the eight germ cells presumably take their reproductive journeys of transformation. Once inside the womb, the eighth ancestor gains knowledge of the Word of the female Nummo, which with the help of the male Nummo takes the shape of a spiraling coil and is transmitted via the womb. This spiraling coil is the textbook image of the DNA molecule with its spiraling coils—the double helix—that we know is the medium of transmission for the genetic "word." The Dogon are again correct that this transmission can only come about with the help of both the female and the male partners. Based on this interpretation of the story, we now understand one reason for the repeated emphasis placed by the Dogon creation story on spiraling coil symbols. Also, the references within the myth to the idea of the word being woven into the cloth represent the chromosomes of DNA, which are the genetic words that are woven into the fabric of each cell. Finally, the story tells us that the eighth ancestor takes fetal form and undergoes an extended period of transformation, which again accurately reflects the next step in the reproductive process, the period of gestation. Each of these images is completely in accordance with what we know from science about the process of sexual reproduction and is presented in a form that could hardly relate to anything but sexual reproduction. Again, this second effort to assign meaning to the Dogon creation symbols results in an organized, factual, and understandable statement about the creation of life and sexual reproduction that is in complete agreement with what a modern encyclopedia would tell us.

In support of this line of interpretation, Griaule and Dieterlen relate some of the sophisticated aspects of Dogon thought as it relates to the reproductive process:

> The children have . . . the same seeds as their parents: those of the father are in a dominant position for a boy and those of the mother for a girl; eight in number and of different "sex," the boy first inherits the "masculine seeds" from his father, which are that same as those of his [male] ancestors, and the daughter the "feminine seeds" of her mother, which are the same as those of her uterine ancestors. Thus, in a symbolism of a biological nature the presence of a double filiation is delineated.[10]

The third theme of the Dogon myths that we will examine is the creation of civilization and is found at the narrative level of the story itself. This story line describes in an organized fashion each of the skills needed to bring a populace of hunters and gatherers to the level of an agrarian society. To do so, the following skills would be needed:

Spoken and written language
The wearing of clothing
The art of weaving

The art of pottery

The skills of agriculture

The skills of metallurgy for making the tools of agriculture

Living in a basic family structure

Organization of a basic framework for community

The skills needed to construct dwellings and storage facilities

In this aspect of the story, the key creation symbols are used as mnemonic devices rather than objects of symbolic meaning. As the narrative progresses, each new skill is presented using the same set of symbols that were previously defined in the myths, and each skill is carefully equated with those previously learned. For example, the movement of the shuttle across the warp during the act of weaving is said to be the same as the motion of the plow across the field in preparation for planting. At the same time, the processes required for mastery of each skill are represented symbolically in the form of commonly found objects, such as the woven garment that a person wears, the configuration of a plowed field, or the granary around which a community is centered. In this way, the trappings of daily life serve as constant reminders of the civilizing skills that have been learned. The Dogon creation myth presents these skills—an arguably essential set of skills—in an orderly and organized sequence, much the same sequence as that in which mankind might possibly have acquired them.

Taken together, these three stories-within-a-story of the Dogon creation myth provide a full and accurate account of the formative processes of the world, of life, and of civilization—just what one would expect to find in a deliberate telling of a story of creation. If true, the meanings we have assigned to the symbols reveal a document that is instructional in nature, a text that could reasonably be interpreted as taught knowledge. Although this kind of interpretation might seem far-fetched, it is one that is actually supported by the ancient myths themselves. Many of the oldest written texts say and most early societies clearly believed that the skills of civilization were taught to mankind by gods or other transcendent beings. So, the pursuit of this line of reasoning is in accordance with what the original texts state. Modern science, however, interprets the surviving documents of these early societies as a blend of mythology and history, and so all such statements have been assigned to the realm of the mythological. However, during the course of the past two centuries, the imaginary line that separates ancient mythology from ancient history has moved slowly and persistently backward in time as new archaeological discoveries cause us to understand as historic what was formerly thought to be mythic.

FIVE

DOGON PARALLELS TO THE BIG BANG AND ATOMIC AND QUANTUM STRUCTURE

The preceding discussion demonstrated many superficial similarities between the surface narrative of the Dogon creation story and the big bang theory of science. However, Griaule and Dieterlen maintained that one of the primary functions of the surface story line of the Dogon is to serve as a kind of mask for a more detailed body of knowledge contained within the deep story line. Therefore, if we are to believe that we are on the right track with our interpretation of Dogon symbols from the surface story line, we should expect to find even more specific and recognizable details of the big bang theory incorporated into the deep story line. In fact, when we carefully examine the elements of the deep story line, this is exactly what we find.

For the Dogon, the starting point for the deep story line is Amma's egg—the mythological counterpart of the unformed universe that contained all of the seeds and signs of the world. According to Dogon mythology, it was the opening of this egg that created all of the spiraling galaxies of stars and worlds. This concept of the origin of the universe conforms nicely to the prevailing theories of astrophysics, which define the unformed universe prior to the Big Bang as a kind of ball containing all of the potential matter of the future universe compressed to an unbelievably dense state. Accordingly, it was the rupturing of this ball that ultimately scattered matter as we now know it to the farthest reaches of the universe. In *Codes of Evolution*, Rush W. Dozier Jr. described the modern concept of the unformed universe as follows:

> Every form of matter, life, and thought that exists today can trace its ancestry through a sequence of earlier forms all the way back to the big bang. The big bang, the echo of which we can still detect as the sea of microwave radiation that fills the universe, is the common ancestor of all things. Evolution began with the big bang. It created space, time, matter, and change: the basic ingredients of unified selection.
>
> Theories of physics suggest that until the big bang there was no space and time as we comprehend the terms. There was no distinction between present and past, and all particles and forces merged into a single, primal field.
>
> The perfect unity that existed at the moment of the big bang has unraveled over the eons. Since the big bang, the overall direction of change in the universe has been one-way: from order to chaos.[1]

As is the case with many of their religious concepts, the Dogon make use of a tangible figure—a carved stone that symbolizes the original primordial egg—to help them visualize their unformed universe. Griaule and Dieterlen described this stone in a passage from *The Pale Fox*:

> This conception of creation is recalled by a figure of the 266 primordial signs schematically drawn under a raised stone. . . . The stone is carved into a slight point (in the form of an egg); it is quadrangular, the corners marking the cardinal directions of the future "opening of Amma's egg."[2]

This physical representation of Amma's egg—a stone with tapered sides that come almost to a point—is reminiscent of the shape of the Dogon granary: conical yet roughly pyramidal. The egg also serves a kind of parallel function to the granary. Just as Amma's egg holds the seeds of the future world, so the Dogon granary holds the seeds of the eight grains of the Dogon. So, both in physical appearance and in function, the granary might be thought of as an alternate rendering of Amma's egg.

According to most astronomers, the perfect unity that existed at the moment of the Big Bang—science's equivalent of Amma's egg— represented a singularity, that is, the point in space-time where both the density of matter and the gravitational field are infinite, forming a black hole. Stephen Hawking described the concept of a black hole in the following way in *A Brief History of Time*:

> John Michell wrote a paper in 1783 in the *Philosophical Transactions of the Royal Society of London* in which he pointed out that a star that was sufficiently massive and compact would have such a strong gravitational field that light could not escape; any light emitted from the surface of the star would be dragged back by the star's gravitational attraction before it could get very far. . . . Such objects are what we now call black holes, because that is what they are: black voids in space. . . . According to theory of relativity, nothing can travel faster than light. Thus if light cannot escape, neither can anything else; everything is dragged back by the gravitational field. So, one has a set of events, a region of space-time, from which it is not possible to escape to reach a distant observer. . . . Its boundary is called the event horizon and coincides with the paths of light rays that just fail to escape from the black hole.[3]

The diagram provided by Hawking to describe the event horizon that is formed by the path of the light rays that are unable to leave a black hole is in most respects the very image of the Dogon stone representing Amma's egg.

In many early mythologies (such as those from Hermopolis in Egypt and from the Maori of New Zealand) the original creation of the universe is linked to the opening of an egg, much like Amma's egg of the

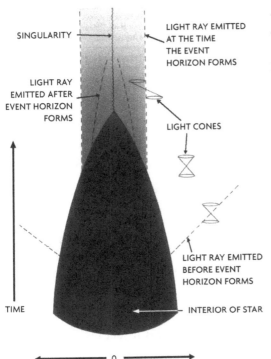

SINGULARITY

LIGHT RAY EMITTED
AT THE TIME
THE EVENT
HORIZON FORMS

LIGHT RAY
EMITTED AFTER
EVENT HORIZON
FORMS

LIGHT CONES

LIGHT RAY EMITTED
BEFORE EVENT
HORIZON FORMS

TIME

INTERIOR OF STAR

0

Left: Diagram of the event horizon of a black hole (from Hawking, A Brief History of Time, *86).*

Below: Dogon rendering of Amma's Egg (from Griaule and Dieterlen, Pale Fox, *361).*

Dogon. The first entities to emerge after the moment of creation are the familiar triad of gods that we previously associated with the three physical states of water. Scientists believe that the plasma that emerged from the Big Bang was intensely hot and cooled rapidly to the near-zero temperature that we now see in the vacuum of space. In a recent article in *Science News* titled "Seeking the Mother of All Matter," this cooling process and its effect on matter in space is described:

> Even as RHIC [Relativistic Heavy Ion Collider] experiments probe the tiniest volumes of space, they also may help scientists make more sense of the biggest thing there is—the universe. As a quark-gluon plasma cools, it condenses into hadrons. This occurs because the inwardly directed pressure of the zero-temperature plasma has taken over, forcing the plasma's constituents back into protons and neutrons. Physicists regard that condensation as a phase transition, like steam becoming water or water freezing into ice.[4]

Prevailing astronomic theory explains that the first finished by-product of this cooling process after the Big Bang was the atom, more specifically the hydrogen atom—the Dogon surface story line's counterpart to the Nummo. Again, if our understanding of the structure of the Dogon religion is correct, we would expect the deep story line of the creation myth to include specific information about the atom and its constituent components, and again in fact it does. We find information about the atom in a section of *The Pale Fox* titled "Creation of the Po." For the Dogon, the po is the name of the "smallest grain," and it represents one of the tiniest building blocks of the universe:

Thus, inside the egg Amma himself was like a spiraling motion, called "accelerated ball," *ogoru gunnu*; then the oval *po* seed was created, which placed itself invisibly at the center. It is said: "When Amma broke the egg of the world and came out, a whirlwind rose. The *po*, which is the smallest (thing), was made, invisible at the center; the wind is Amma himself. It is the *po* which Amma let come out first." Amma's creative will was located in the *po*, the smallest of things. Like a central air bubble, it spun and scattered the particles of matter in a sonorous and luminous motion which, however, remained inaudible and invisible. It was less a word than a thought . . . the *po* is the image of the origin of matter. Therefore, it will later be forbidden for different categories of men to . . . speak about it; because "the beginning of things is Amma's greatest secret." Moreover, the *po* is also the image of the creator.

"Amma, the creator, was not himself great (big), but of that it is forbidden to speak. . . . Amma, from the moment when he created all things, each was like the *po*; they grew larger whereas the *po* did not; the seed was formed like the wind and it is forbidden to talk about it."

The seed is . . . called *po*, a word considered to have the same root as *polo*, "beginning." Indeed, due to its smallness, it is the image of the beginning of all things. "All of the things that Amma created begin like the little (seed of) *po*." And, beginning with this

infinitely small thing, the things created by Amma will form themselves by continuous addition of identical elements; "Amma makes
things begin (by creating them as) small (as the) *po*; he continues to
add (to the things created) little by little. . . . As Amma adds . . . the
thing becomes large."[5]

Dogon descriptions of the po at the opening of Amma's egg, forming like a central air bubble and scattering in a luminous motion, correlate well with scientific descriptions of the process of the cooling of
the quark-gluon plasma. If we read on further in the previously cited
Science News article, it states, "It's common during phase transitions,
like water's familiar ones, for bubbles of unchanged matter to linger and
then suddenly and violently burst in a belated transformation into the
new phase."[6]

Clearly, what is being spoken of in the above passages is the formation of the building blocks of matter—atoms and their components.
So, when we suggest possible meanings for the Dogon symbols that are
related to atomic structure, the idea is wholly and completely in keeping
with how the Dogon understand their own symbols. (In *Dictionnaire
Dogon*, Genevieve Calame-Griaule describes the po as "the image of
the atom."[7]) However, if we look carefully, we can see that the surface
story of the Dogon myth might also pointedly direct us to the concepts
of quantum physics. Imagine for a moment that you must read an article
written in a foreign language that, for the most part, you do not understand. Then imagine that two words you do understand, *supply and
demand*, are repeated again and again within the passage. It would not
take the insight of a genius to surmise that the subject of the article might
be economics. The Dogon creation story provides us with a similar clue
to its meaning with its recurring emphasis on pellets of clay and spiraling
coils. It requires only a little imagination to see these symbols as likely
references to particles and waves—the essential building blocks of quantum theory. We find a good description of this dual nature of quantum
particles in Richard P. Feynman's *The Character of Physical Law*:

Electrons, when they were first discovered, behaved exactly like particles or bullets, very simply. Further research showed, from electron diffraction experiments for example, that they behaved like waves. As time went on there was a growing confusion about how these things really behaved—waves or particles, particles or waves? Everything looked like both.

This growing confusion was resolved in 1925 or 1926 with the advent of correct equations for quantum mechanics. Now we know how the electrons and light behave. But what can I call it? If I say they behave like particles, I give the wrong impression; also if I say they behave like waves. They behave in their own inimitable way, which technically could be called a quantum mechanical way.[8]

Within the creation story we can see an implied knowledge of the wave properties of physics when the Dogon say that the fibers of the first garment mimic the sound of the voice of the Nummo, which tapers off in spiraling coils—a statement that betrays an understanding by the teller of the creation story that sound travels in waves.

If we look more deeply into the subject of quantum physics, we learn about a fundamental principle, called the exclusion principle, which states that no two electrons can occupy the same quantum, or energy, state of an atom at the same time. The quantum state of an electron is defined by four mathematical values called quantum numbers. So, if we return to our first interpretation of the Dogon creation story, in which the Nummo pair represents the electrons of hydrogen, the science of quantum physics brings us right back to our same Dogon number symbols, two and eight—which in this case represent the two electrons and their eight quantum numbers. A little further inquiry into the subject tells us that not only electrons but also the protons and neutrons in the nucleus of an atom are bound by a fundamental limit that allows only two per quantum orbit, and those two must be of opposite spins. These requirements of science speak to two fundamental notions of the Dogon creation story—the principle in the universe of twin births and the inherent pairing of male and female, in this instance represented as the positive charge of the proton and the negative charge of the electron.

The next key concept of quantum physics that we should examine is Heisenberg's uncertainty principle, which declares that it is not possible to know both the exact position of an electron and its momentum at the same instant. The reason for this is that physicists learn about the nature of quantum particles through inference—that is, not through direct observation but by deliberately bouncing other particles off them. However, because these particles are so very small and lightweight, any collision with another particle will necessarily disturb their position or momentum. Consequently, a scientist can determine the precise position of a quantum particle or its precise momentum, but not both at the same moment.

Unlikely as it may seem, this principle of quantum physics brings us to an interesting puzzle relating to both Dogon granaries and pyramids. Among the ancient civilizations of the world, we find two basic types of pyramids—those with flat tops and those that come to a peak. We can find examples of both varieties of pyramid among the symbols of the Egyptian religion, but in Dogon mythology we are told only about the flat-topped granary. Yet there is an unusual discrepancy within the Dogon mythology itself pertaining to the granary and its physical shape. The Dogon creation myth provides us with specific dimensions for the structure of the granary, including a round base with a diameter of 20 cubits, four 10-step staircases (one per side) with steps measuring 1 cubit high and 1 cubit deep, rising to a square, flat top measuring 8 cubits per side. However, when we actually apply these dimensions to a model in which the steps are inset as part of the face (as would be the case with a step pyramid), we are left with a basic contradiction in the dimensions.

If we restrict ourselves to a base with a diameter of 20 cubits, four stairways with 10 steps 1 cubit high and 1 cubit deep would meet at nearly a peak, leaving a square of only 2 cubits per side at the top of the granary. In order to build a model with a square, flat top of sides measuring 8 cubits, we would either have to reduce the number of steps to six per side or move the base of each stairway several cubits out from the circular edge of the granary. In other words, we can place the staircases

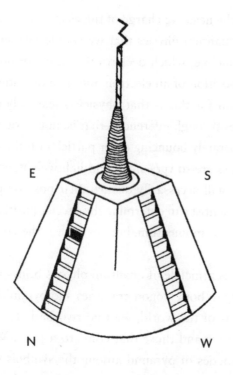

The plan of the Dogon granary, or world-system plan (from Griaule, Conversations with Ogotemmeli, *33).*

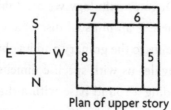

Plan of upper story

Ground plan

in the right location or include the correct number of steps, but not both. This quandary is of precisely the same nature as the uncertainty principle of quantum theory (in which both the precise location and momentum of a particle cannot be known simultaneously) and expresses itself mathematically in terms of the number of steps in four staircases, the same as the number of values needed to define the quantum state of an electron.

In *The Pale Fox,* Griaule and Dieterlen describe a basic approach to the act of creating that is defined within the framework of Dogon mythology. This approach includes four phases or stages and, for the Dogon, applies equally to any creative project, whether it be a creative act of Amma or an undertaking of man—for example, the building of a dwelling. The first of these is the conceptual stage, in which an idea is conceived, and which the Dogon call *bummo.* At this stage, the project exists only in signs or seeds—symbols that represent the final thing to be created. For a middle school student assigned to write a report, this would be the equivalent of selecting a topic. In the second stage, called the *yala,* the project is conceptualized in broad strokes that identify the boundaries of the object to be created. This compares roughly to our middle school student's report outline. Griaule and Dieterlen described this phase in *The Pale Fox:*

> After the first series, that of abstract signs or "trace" *bummo,* will come the second series, that of the *yala* "mark" or "image," exe- cuted in dotted lines. . . . "The *yala* of a thing is like the beginning of the thing." Therefore, when one builds a house, one delineates the foundation with stones placed at the corners: these stones are the *yala,* the "marks" of the future dwelling. The term *yala* also has the meaning of "reflection," which expresses the future form of the thing represented.[9]

The third developmental stage refines the image of the thing to be created by filling in the main details of the object or concept. We could say that this third stage would be comparable to a student's detailed notes or perhaps to a first draft of the report. In regard to this stage, Griaule and Dieterlen wrote:

> The third series of signs is that of the *tonu*, "figure," "diagram," or sometimes "periphery," of things. The *tonu* is a schematic outline of generally separated graphic elements; it is the sketch, the rough draft of the thing or being represented. The word *tonu* comes from *tono*, "to portray," which also means "to begin," but in the dynamic sense of the word. It is said that Amma "began things," *amma kize tono,* to demonstrate the initial impetus he gave to creation. . . . The *tonu* of the house connotes the pebbles that have been placed between the corner- stones to delimit the walls.[10]

The fourth and final stage of the creative act is to produce the finished image of the thing to be created. It is interesting that the Dogon make almost no distinction between the representation of an object and the object itself. Griaule and Dieterlen described this completion stage in *The Pale Fox:*

> The fourth series consists of the "drawings," *toymu* (or *toy*), as realistically representative of the thing as possible. It is also the thing itself. When one has finished the building of a house, it is as if one had made a complete drawing, *toymu,* of the house. In speaking of the *toy* and of Amma, one says: "To make the drawing is to make the thing that he (Amma) has in mind. It is, therefore, to represent the thing created in its reality."[11]

The example of building a house is an interesting one for Griaule and Dieterlen to have selected to illustrate the creative process because it reveals the creation myth as a likely source of architectural knowledge. In fact, the four-step process from bummo to yala to tonu to toy is very similar to the process taught to modern students of architectural drawing—first conceiving a structure, then defining with point marks the outer boundaries of a structure, then marking in greater detail the other structural features, and finally creating a finished drawing. Like-wise, it is similar to the usual modern approach to construction itself, in which a site is surveyed, oriented, and staked before any actual construction work begins. Most importantly, it represents a basic organizational mindset of the sort needed for any person or culture to advance successfully.

As we examine the Dogon symbols as they relate to quantum physics, we should note that the four creative stages of the Dogon—bummo, yala, tonu, and toy—might have bearing on another set of concepts from quantum physics relating to the four types of force-carrying particles. Hawking described these particles and their relationship to the building blocks of atoms in *A Brief History of Time:*

> Force-carrying particles can be grouped into four categories according to the strength of the force that they carry and the particles with which they interact. . . . The first category is the gravitational force. This force is universal, that is, every particle feels the force of gravity, according to its mass or energy. . . . [T]he force between two matter particles is pictured as being carried by a particle . . . called the graviton. . . . [G]ravitons . . . are very weak—and so difficult to detect that they have never yet been observed.
>
> The next category is the electromagnetic force, which interacts with electrically charged particles like electrons. . . . The electromagnetic attraction between negatively charged electrons and positively charged protons in the nucleus causes the electrons to orbit the nucleus of the atom.
>
> The third category is called the weak nuclear force. . . . [This force] exhibits a property known as spontaneous symmetry breaking. This means that what appear to be a number of completely different particles at low energies are in fact found to be all the same type of particle, only in different states. . . . The effect is rather like the behaviour of a roulette ball on a roulette wheel. At high energies (when the wheel is spun quickly) the ball behaves essentially in only one way—it rolls round and round. But

as the wheel slows, the energy of the ball decreases, and eventually the ball drops into one of the thirty-seven slots in the wheel.

The fourth category is the strong nuclear force, which holds the quarks together in the proton and neutron, and holds the protons and neutrons together in the nucleus of the atom.[12]

These particles, as Hawking describes them, follow the same pattern as the bummo, yala, tonu, and toy: The graviton is so weak and undetectable as to be a concept. The electromagnetic force defines the outline of the object. The weak nuclear force at states of high energy refines the component particles into an approximation of one particle, and the strong nuclear force binds, or "draws," the atom.

According to the Dogon, the po seed—already one of the most basic elements of creation—consists of four even more elemental components, referred to in combination as the sene seed, described by Griaule and Dieterlen:

> In this infinitely small thing Amma then placed the four elements which thus far had contained the four *tonu* of the *sene*. . . . The *sene* represents the first thing created by Amma. . . . Amma's acts are represented by a series of figures. The first, called "diagram of the *sene seed*" . . . connotes the superposition of the four elements in the formation of the seed. . . . In accordance with Amma's will, each of them extended its "germ" to touch its neighbor, from east to north, from north to west, etc. This "crossing of the germs" is compared to the intertwining of twigs forming a "nest," *senu*. These germs then gathered at the center, where they mixed together and were transformed at the very site of the *po*, which was still invisible. Then, surrounding the seed, they made it visible.[13]

This "crossing of the germs" in all directions would appear even to the nontechnical observor to be a description of the electrons in their crossing orbits surrounding a nucleus. These orbiting electrons, combined with their nucleus—the po—constitute a completed atom.

Within *The Pale Fox,* Griaule and Dieterlen present a Dogon diagram of the *sene* seed that is a close match for typical scientific diagrams showing normal electron density and electron orbital shapes. Compare the scientific diagram reproduced below with the Dogon drawing beneath it as rendered in *The Pale Fox*:

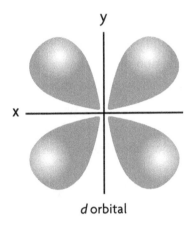

d orbital

Electron orbit shape. One of the typical shapes an electron traces as it orbits the nucleus of an atom.

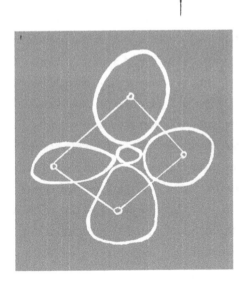

Dogon drawing of the sene
(from Griaule and Dieterlen, The Pale Fox, *135).*

The shape of the electron orbit diagram is based on mathematical calculations of the most probable location of electrons as they orbit around a nucleus. However, the shape of the orbit itself is far from being theoretical. It has been verified by many scientific experiments and validated by actual images produced by electron microscopes.

Based on this interpretation, the sene of the Dogon would represent components of an atom: electrons, protons, and neutrons. Yet the Dogon also speak about the germination of the sene, which from this point of view would mean the creation of electrons, protons, and neutrons from smaller particles. What this suggests is that for us to understand the Dogon symbols for the germination of the sene, it could only be helpful to know more about atomic particles. For this explanation, we turn again to the comments of Stephen Hawking in *A Brief History of Time*:

> Using the wave/particle duality . . . everything in the universe, including light and gravity, can be described in terms of particles. These particles have a property called spin. One way of thinking of spin is to imagine the particles as little tops spinning about an axis. However, this can be misleading, because quantum mechanics tells us that the particles do not have any well-defined axis. What the spin of a particle really tells us is what the particle looks like from different directions. A particle of spin 0 . . . looks the same from every direction. On the other hand, a particle of spin 1 is like an arrow: it looks different from different directions. Only if one turns it round a complete revolution (360 degrees) does the particle look the same. A particle of spin 2 is like a double-headed arrow: it looks the same if one turns it round half a revolution (180 degrees) . . . but the remarkable fact is that there are particles that do not look the same if one turns them through just one revolution: you have to turn them through two complete revolutions! Such particles are said to have a spin of $1/2$.[14]

Hawking's description from quantum physics provides us with an exceptionally workable caption for the following Dogon diagram of the germination of the sene, also taken from *The Pale Fox*:

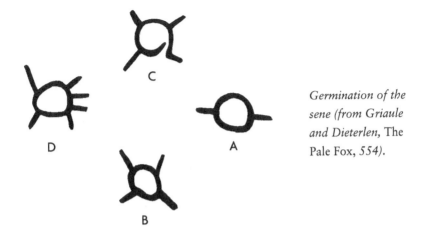

Germination of the sene (from Griaule and Dieterlen, The Pale Fox, *554).*

Figure B in the above diagram calls to mind Hawking's particle with a spin value of 0. From a two-dimensional perspective based on four cardinal points, it looks the same from all directions. Figure C resembles a particle with a spin value of 1—it must be turned 360 degrees in order to look the same. Figure A corresponds to a particle with a spin value of 2—it needs only be turned 180 degrees to look the same. The very odd layout of figure D seems to be an attempt—obviously not possible in two dimensions—to represent a particle with a spin value of $1/2$, which requires two full 360-degree turns to look the same.

In relation to these particles, Hawking also stated: "All the known particles in the universe can be divided into two groups: particles of spin $1/2$, which make up the matter in the universe, and particles of spin 0, 1, and 2, which . . . give rise to forces between the matter particles."[15]

Although the Dogon diagram cannot accurately portray the $1/2$ spin particle, the author of the Dogon creation story came up with an inventive way of describing it, once again using the symbol of the granary—the same symbol previously used to represent other concepts of quantum physics. This interpretation begins with the assignment of a set of values to the sene particles that reaffirm their identification as the components of matter of all variety. Griaule and Dieterlen wrote the following description in *The Pale Fox:*

Having thought and then designed the world he wished to create, Amma tried as an experiment to superimpose a bit of every kind of substance. . . . The result of this first labor was the seed of the tree *sene na*. . . . The oval-shaped seed . . . had to contain four elements. . . . It is said that in order to create the *sene na*, Amma "cleared his throat, which made earth; his saliva became water; he breathed when he returned to the sky, this being fire; he blew hard, this being wind. He did not mix the elements, but superposed them: he put down earth, then water, then fire, then air." Amma, to create the *sene na*, superposed things separated into four.[16]

In this way, the symbolic interpretation was assigned that all matter is created from the four elements of Earth, Water, Fire, and Wind—symbols that were actually associated with the four types of quantum particles but were apparently taken by the Greeks to be the actual components of all matter. Based on this symbolism, we now understand that when Dogon mythology speaks of fire, it might actually be in reference to a quantum particle. This knowledge provides us with the necessary key to understand the otherwise obscure Dogon tale of the stolen fire of the smithy—a tale that supports the notion that the Greeks knew of these same symbols because of its parallels to the Greek myth of Prometheus, who was said to have stolen fire from the gods. Griaule related this story in *Conversations with Ogotemmeli*:

All was now ready . . . except that there was no fire in the smithy. The ancestor slipped into the workshop of the great Nummo, who are Heaven's smiths, and stole a piece of the sun in the form of live embers and white-hot iron. He seized it by means of a "robbers stick" the crook of which ended in a slit, open like a mouth. He dropped some of the embers, came back to pick them up, and fled towards the granary; but his agitation was such that he could no longer find the entrances. He made the round of it several times before he found the steps and climbed to the flat roof, where he hid the stolen goods in one of the skins of the bellows, exclaiming: "*Gouyo!*" which is to say, "Stolen."[17]

On the surface, this story makes absolutely no sense because we know that the granary had four staircases to the top, so the ancestor should not have had to circle it even once to find steps to the top. However, we know from the symbolism of the sene that fire is one of the symbols of the quantum elements, from which all matter is made. The act of circling the granary more than once to get back to the start is a reference to the double turn (720 degrees) required to return a $1/2$ spin particle back to its starting point. The symbolism of the word "stolen" is a reference to electrons—a subparticle that is made from a $1/2$ spin particle and that science tells us is stolen from one atom by another in order to form a molecular bond. Furthermore, Hawking tells us:

> Modern nuclear theory is based on the notion that nuclei consist of neutrons and protons that are held together by extremely powerful "nuclear" forces. The elucidation of these nuclear forces requires physicists to disrupt neutrons and protons by bombarding nuclei with extremely energetic particles. Such bombardments have revealed more than 200 so-called elementary particles, or tiny bits of matter, most of which exist for much less than one hundred-millionth of a second.[18]

When Hawking speaks of the existence of "more than 200" elementary particles, he implies that there are more types of particles to be found, as yet undiscovered or unconfirmed by modern science. This approximate number of particles—expected by Hawking to increase—correlates well with the Dogon figure of 266 seeds or signs. Griaule and Dieterlen went on to tell us that these 266 signs are classified into alternate groupings by the Dogon:

> Moreover, Amma's 266 *bummo*, of which we have seen the basic division into 8, are also classified in the following manner: 6, then

20, then 4 times 60. During the sowing celebration, when the sacrifice is offered on the altar called *manna amma,* "Amma of the
sky," the Arou priest says: "Amma's number is 266; it begins with
6 *bummo* to which are added 20; 4 times 60 more; Amma made
6 *bummo* of things in the beginning; he added 20 (then) placed
4 times 60 more *(bummo).* These two ways denote a division
in base 8, female, and a division in base 6, male. This expresses
that the *bummo,* symbol of Amma's creative thought, contains in
essence—by the specific value of the number, another fundamental
expression of the groundwork of creation—sexual twinness, male
and female, which will be at the base of the realization in matter of
divine thought."[19]

The first six bummo of Amma's creation, already identified among
the 266 signs as quantum particles, are easily recognized as the six varieties of quarks as described by Hawking:

There are a number of different varieties of quarks: there are
thought to be at least six "flavors," which we call up, down,
strange, charmed, bottom, and top. Each flavor comes in three
"colors," red, green and blue. (It should be emphasized that these
terms are just labels; quarks are much smaller than the wavelength
of visible light and so do not have any color in the normal sense.
It is just that modern physicists seem to have more imaginative
ways of naming new particles and phenomena—they no longer
restrict themselves to Greek!) A proton or neutron is made up of
three quarks, one of each color. A proton contains two up quarks
and one down quark; a neutron contains two down quarks and
one up.[20]

Based on the preceding diagrams and the descriptions by Hawking
of the elemental particles and forces involved with quantum mechanics,
we can see that the symbolism in the Dogon deep story line relating to
the 266 signs or seeds of Amma presents a stunningly accurate portrait

of the component building blocks of matter as we presently know them. On the other hand, if the Dogon count of 266 elementary particles ultimately turns out to be the correct scientific number, then the Dogon creation story might well have drawn the meanings of its symbols from a body of scientific knowledge that actually goes a bit beyond our own.

SIX

DOGON PARALLELS TO STRING THEORY

G iven the extraordinary correspondence between the Dogon symbols of the po and the sene to their counterparts within basic quantum theory, it makes sense to pursue this correspondence one level deeper by examining the structure of the quantum particles themselves. To make this comparison, we must look to the theory of superstrings, a promising but as yet unverifiable theory of what might be the last indivisible component particles of matter. String theory came to the forefront of scientific thought in the early 1980s, and although verification of certain key aspects of this theory remain beyond our technological grasp, it continues to be the most viable candidate for a unified theory of the universe. Brian Greene explained the basis of the theory in his 1999 book *The Elegant Universe:*

> [Quantum] particles are the "letters" of all matter. Just like their linguistic counterparts, they appear to have no further internal substructure. String theory proclaims otherwise. According to string theory, if we could examine these particles with even greater precision—a precision many orders of magnitude beyond our present technological capacity—we would find that each is not pointlike, but instead consists of a tiny one dimensional *loop*. Like an infinitely thin rubber

band, each particle contains a vibrating, oscillating, dancing filament that physicists . . . have named a *string*.[1]

Greene went on to explain this tiny realm of matter in more detail:

[In string theory,] all properties of the microworld are within the realm of its explanatory power. To understand this, let's first think about more familiar strings, such as those on a violin. Each such string can undergo a huge variety (in fact, infinite in number) of different vibrational patterns known as *resonances*. . . . These are the wave patterns whose peaks and troughs are evenly spaced and fit perfectly between the string's two fixed endpoints. Our ears sense the different resonant vibrational patterns as different musical notes. The strings in string theory have similar properties. There are resonant vibrational patterns that the string can support by virtue of their evenly spaced peaks and troughs exactly fitting along its spacial extent. . . . Just as the different vibrational patterns of a violin string give rise to different musical notes, *the different vibrational patterns of a fundamental string give rise to the different masses and force charges*.[2]

As a visual aid to understanding strings, Greene included diagrams of several of these vibrational patterns:

Vibratory pattern of a string (from Greene, The Elegant Universe, *145).*

As we continue with our interpretation of the Dogon symbols that could correspond to these strings, we realize that any discussion of components more fundamental than those used in the germination of the sene brings us to the level of the 266 seeds or signs of Amma. In regard to these signs, Griaule stated in his article, "The Dogon," that the Dogon "conception of the universe is based . . . on a principle of vibrations of matter."[3] This basis for the Dogon structure of matter is reaffirmed by a Dogon drawing that describes the 266 seeds or signs. Griaule and Dieterlen's description of a Dogon planting ritual in *The Pale Fox* provides more evidence:

> The creation and the picture of the signs are also commemorated annually before sowing *(bado)* by the following ritual. Early in the morning the head of the family goes to the "field of the ancestors," *vageu minne,* and clears a neat area at the center for making the signs. On this spot he then places a *tazu* basket upside down to draw a circle, which will bear the same name as the altar of the field: then he makes a pile of stones, *sogo.* Facing the east, he first draws on the ground a small circle about 12 cm. in diameter inside the first circle, with a dot in the center. In the course of that day, he makes a zigzag line around the inner circle, repeating this twenty-two times, so as to fill the outer circle with an intricate tangle of lines representing all possible signs. . . . One says of this gesture: "The 266 (signs) are drawn in the center of the field of the ancestors."[4]

In place of a photograph of this field drawing, Griaule and Dieterlen presented what they called a "theoretical diagram" of this drawing, which compares favorably with Greene's vibrational examples. Together, the Dogon field drawing along with Griaule's statement about the vibrational nature of matter firmly link the Dogon symbols to their counterparts in string theory. We know that quantum science assigns the source of these vibrations of matter to a string. It is therefore significant that, for the Dogon, the component structure that would equate to a

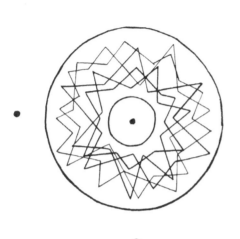

*Dogon field drawing
(from Griaule and
Dieterlen,* The Pale Fox,
108).

string is a thread, one that is said to be the work of the spider of the sene.
Griaule and Dieterlen wrote, "Now the spider *dada yurugu geze gezene*
(literally: '*dada* who holds the thread of the Fox') had been delegated
by Amma . . . it entered the *sene na* . . . in order to 'weave the words'
of Ogo."[5]

Although a string is many times smaller than the smallest particle
that can be imaged by present-day scientists, the Dogon retain a clear
sense of what their primordial thread looks like. Griaule and Dieterlen
included a Dogon diagram of the "work of the spider in the sene" (seen
below) in an appendix to *The Pale Fox:*

Based on the preceding discussion, we can see a continued correlation between Dogon symbols and the deep theoretical science of string

*Work of the spider in the
sene (from Griaule and
Dieterlen,* The Pale Fox,
554).

theory. However, in this one instance, the drawing of the Dogon thread presents us with a significant difference between what science proposes as theory and what the Dogon state as fact. The Dogon tell us that the underlying strings of matter are found in coils, not in loops.

Dogon mythology provides us with other important similarities that help confirm the correlation between the thread of the Dogon spider and the strings of science. For one, just as the strings of string theory are thought to give rise to the four quantum forces—gravity, the electromagnetic force, the weak nuclear force, and the strong nuclear force—the Dogon tell us that the spider of the sene also "gives birth" to four sene seeds:

> The four branches of the *sene na* in which the spider was working will bear fruit. . . . The first seed caught by the *sene* was that of the *mono,* a word meaning "to bring together." . . . [The second] *sene gommuzo* or "bumpy"; *sene benu* or "stocky"; *sene urio* that bows (its head). The four *sene* will embody on earth the four *yala* allocated to the *sene na* seed in Amma's womb, which contained the four elements in this order: *sene na,* water; *sene gommuzo,* air; *sene benu,* fire; *sene urio,* earth.[6]

Like the strings that produce what modern science sees as quantum particles, the thread of the spider of the sene "gives birth" to the four previously identified categories of quantum particles. Many of the specific attributes of string theory vary, depending upon how likely scientists determine it is for a single string to split apart or two strings to join into one. This likelihood is defined by a numerical value called the string coupling constant. The lower the value of the constant, the more strings behave like one-dimensional threads. The higher the value, the more they behave like two-dimensional membranes. Greene wrote, "The fundamental ingredient of theory appears to be a one-dimensional string . . . however . . . if we . . . turn the value of the respective string coupling constants up . . . what appeared to be one-dimensional strings stretch into two-dimensional membranes."[7]

According to Griaule and Dieterlen, the Dogon's spiraling components of matter exhibit similar behavior. In the chapter of *The Pale Fox* titled "The Work of the Po Pilu," they wrote the following:

> The spiral of things that were rolled up in the *po* . . . represent the name given by Amma. The names were first put inside the *po*; while whirling about, it created a bond between one thing and the thing after it. In this way, the names formed a sort of thin covering (compared to the one surrounding the brain); by spinning around, this "skin" became like a tube containing things in series.[8]

One current version of string theory, called M-theory, defines a universe that consists of eleven dimensions—four that we can detect (height, width, length, time) and seven that we cannot detect. A good example to help conceptualize one of these undetectable dimensions— borrowed from Greene's *The Elegant Universe*—is to imagine an ant walking along a high-tension power line. From a distance, the power line seems to have only one dimension—the ant can only walk forward or backward. However, when viewed up close, one can see that the ant can actually move in another previously unseen direction—in a circle around the power line. In an article titled "String Theory and M-Theory," Markus Basan and Claus Basan described how these dimensions work:

> In M-theory on every point in four dimensional space-time there is a tiny curled up Calabi-Yau space of seven dimensions. All dimensions are closed. . . . After the Big Bang only 4 dimensions expanded while the other 7 remained curled up. They are so small that they are impossible for us to see or detect. The strings vibrate in this 7D bundle. . . . To produce new Calabi-Yau spaces, space can tear and repair itself after curving in another way. One can prove that the new shapes cannot be created without the tearing.[9]

In the drawing below, we can see how Dogon mythology provides similar details on how a string evolves in this seven-dimensional space:

Development inside the seed
(from Griaule and Dieterlen, The Pale Fox, *137).*

Dogon mythological descriptions provided by Griaule and Dieterlen of how matter evolves inside the seed continue to run parallel to the scientific processes of string theory as described by Greene:

> The development of life inside the seed is represented by a series of figures called "drawings of the multiplication of the word of the *po,*" which suggests the successive appearance of seven vibrations developing in star-shaped fashion around a central nucleus. . . . The . . . figures show the development of the vibrations in segments of increasing size, ending with the seventh (at left). . . . Their extremities are at progressively greater distance from the center. As a result, these extremities are on a spiral comparable to that of the *yala* of the *po.* The development of the seed can take place only on the outside after the seventh segment had gone thorough the "wall" of the egg; because of this, it split up to form an eighth element. . . . In this way, the eighth articulation of the "word" within the seed will also have the privilege of being the germ of the first in a new being.[10]

These details relating to the primordial thread of the Dogon bring the mythological portrait of matter to completion. The narrative of the Dogon creation story begins with Amma's egg, represented as a black hole, then describes the atom, and takes us through each stage of matter all the way down to massless particles or strings. However, Greene reminded us that, implicit within string theory itself is an intimate link between black holes and massless particles that is best described by our mythological triad of gods that relate to the three states of water:

> The connection between black holes and elementary particles . . . is closely akin to something we are all familiar with from day-to-day life, known technically as phase transition. A simple example of a phase transition is the one we mentioned: . . . water can exist as a solid (ice), as a liquid (liquid water), and a gas (steam). These are known as the *phases* of water, and the transformation from one form to another is called a *phase transition*. . . . Again, just as someone who has never before encountered liquid water or solid ice would not immediately recognize that they are two phases of the same underlying substance, physicists had not realized [before string theory] that the kinds of black holes we were studying and elementary particles are actually two phases of the same underlying stringy material.[11]

In essence, Dogon cosmology seems to describe the true underlying structure of matter, organizes it in the right sequence, diagrams it correctly, and assigns the correct attributes to each of its components. Moreover, it does so within the explicit context of a discussion of the structure of matter. One of the underlying principles of science—called Occam's razor—states that, all other considerations being equal, we should prefer the simplest answer to any given scientific problem. In this case, hard though it may be to conceive, the simplest answer might well be that the Dogon myths do, in fact, describe the components of matter they so strongly resemble. Given the close and consistent correlation between Dogon descriptions, symbols, and drawings and those of science, any alternative suggestion of mere coincidence would seem to somehow strain the very definition of the word "coincidence."

SEVEN

DOGON PARALLELS TO EGYPTIAN MYTHOLOGY

The many persistent similarities between Dogon and Egyptian religious symbols and lifestyles lead to a natural suggestion that modern Dogon society could actually represent a modern remnant of ancient Egyptian culture. Up to this point in our discussion, we have mentioned several superficial aspects of commonality between the two societies that tend to support this idea. However, if Dogon stories and symbols are to be truly understood as surviving artifacts of such an exceedingly ancient tradition, then we ought to be able to equate many of the most essential Dogon concepts and symbols with specific counterparts in Egyptian mythology and religion. Perhaps the most direct method for accomplishing this is to review similar elements of Egyptian religion in the same context and sequence as they are presented by the storylines of the Dogon creation myth.

The surface story line of the Egyptian religion begins with the god Amen, a likely equivalent to the Dogon god Amma in name, attributes, and actions. Unlike the Dogon religion, Egyptian mythology often produced a wealth of alternate names for any given god or goddess. Many times—as in the case of the Egyptian god Ra—these aliases have been interpreted by modern scholars as expressions of various aspects of the god.[1] Over the tens of centuries of Egyptian history, many alternate names evolved for the god Amen, including that of Atum, who was the head of the Egyptian pantheon of gods in dynastic times and heir to Amen's attributes and icons. Some of these names take the form of homonyms, anagrams, and shortened or expanded versions of the name Amen. Godfrey Higgins, a nineteenth century writer and Hebrew scholar with no apparent knowledge of the Dogon religion, notes in his 1833 work *Anacalypsis* that if the letters of the Hebrew word *omun*—a rough homonym of *Amen*—are reversed, the resulting word is "Numo."[2] Perhaps the earliest incarnation of Amen, which predates even the beginning of writing in Egypt, is the god Min, whose icon is described as a meteoric stone not unlike the carved Dogon stone that represents Amma's egg. Another equivalent name for Amen is held by the lesser-known Egyptian god Nemmhu, whose name is a close phonetic match both for the Dogon Nummo and the Sumerian mother goddess Nammu. Another, more prominent Egyptian pseudonym for Amen and Min is that of the Egyptian god Menu—again a recognizable near-anagram of Nemmhu and also the name of an important god in the ancient traditions of India. Menu has additional importance for this study because his hieroglyphic name consists of characters that represent the key symbols of the Dogon creation story: water, a spiraling coil, a clay pot, the sun, and a drawing board:

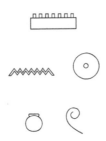

The Egyptian tendency to use words that sound alike as a way to associate the true meanings of religious concepts was explained with great clarity by Serge Sauneron in his book *The Priests of Ancient Egypt:*

The Egyptians never considered their language—that corresponding to the hieroglyphs—as a *social* tool; for them, it always remained a resonant echo of the vital energy that had brought the universe to life, a *cosmic* force. Thus, study of this language enabled them to "explain" the cosmos.

It was word-play that served as the means of making these explanations. The moment one understands that words are intimately linked to the essences of the beings or objects they indicate, resemblances between words cannot be fortuitous; they express a natural relationship, a subtle connection that priestly erudition would have to define. . . .

This practice can seem childish and anything but serious. Yet its logic emerges if we try to understand the value the Egyptians placed on the pronunciation of words. Any superficial resemblance between two words was understood as conveying a direct connection between the two entities invoked. It thus became a general practice, employed in all periods and in all areas of inquiry, and in priestly lore it was the basic technique for explaining proper nouns, essentially the very means of defining the nature of the deities. This was the case with Amun, the great patron of Thebes. We do not know just what his name meant, but it was pronounced like another word meaning "to be hidden," and the scribes played on this resemblance to define Amun as the great god who hid his real appearance from his children. . . . The mere similarity of the sounds of the two words was enough to arouse a suspicion on the part of the priests that there was some close relationship between them, and to find in it an explanation of the god's name: "thus addressing the primordial god . . . as an invisible and hidden being, they invite him and exhort him, calling him Amun, to show and reveal himself."[3]

Some researchers—such as James. P. Allen in his *An Introduction to the Language and Culture of the Hieroglyphs*—interpreted Egyptian wordplay as a fondness for puns and suggest that the priests deliberately used them to disguise references to the innermost secrets of the Egyptian religion. In *The Sirius Mystery*, Robert K. G. Temple provided examples of what he saw as Egyptian puns and some of the difficulties they present to translators and researchers:

> It should be noted that in Egyptian the hieroglyph *tchet* of a serpent means both "serpent" and "body." The cobra hieroglyph *ara* means both "serpent" and "goddess." Elsewhere we encounter *ara* frequently having the common general meaning of "goddess." The frequent incorporation of the serpent into late Sirius-lore among the Greeks probably stems from a pun or corruption of the Egyptian determinative form for "goddess." . . . [I]n fact, if an Egyptian were to write "the Goddess Sirius" in hieroglyphs, the result . . . [could] also (by pun) be read quite literally as "serpent's tooth." . . . In short, when does a pun cease to be a pun and merely consist of a mistranslation based on ignorance of the true subject-matter?[4]

To define these priestly "second meanings" as puns might not entirely do justice to the way in which they were used. Like the Egyptians, the Dogon also assign double meanings to words and phrases that are important to their religion. As an illustrative example, consider again the name of the Dogon creation story, aduno so tanie, which can mean "astonishing myth of the universe" or "secret symbols." Either phrase alone makes a correct statement about the Dogon creation story, but both statements together provide a much more exact definition of the creation story and how it works. This technique of using multiple meanings serves to disguise the full import of a concept from the uninitiated while at the same time enhancing a broader definition for the initiated.

There is a tradition among ancient mythologies that if you were to learn the true name of a god, you would acquire power over that god. However, given the way the Egyptian and Dogon languages work, one is led to suspect that this tradition has more to do with secret meanings than with actual secret names. The Egyptian phrase *bu maa*, which is translated as "truth," actually implies something that is a "longstanding perception" or something that has been "thoroughly examined." The Egyptian word *maa* means "to perceive or examine"—therefore the word *maat,* defined by Budge as meaning "truth" or "justice" would literally mean "that which has been perceived or examined."[5] The Egyptian word *bu* is used as a name for Amen—the timeless and infinite god. *Dictionnaire Dogon* tells us that the Dogon word *bu* means "timeless, endless, or infinite." Consequently, a "thoroughly examined word or phrase" is one for which all of the multiple meanings are known, thereby providing true knowledge of—and power over—the concept it represents.

While the similarities of deity names previously discussed allow us to draw suggestive parallels between gods of different cultures—like the Dogon Nummo and the Egyptian Khnum—we also find support for these proposed relationships in the icons associated with these gods. For instance, in Egyptian hieroglyphs, the name of the god Khnum can be rendered by one of the central symbols from the Dogon myths, the image of a simple clay pot:

In Egyptian mythology, Khnum was credited with having created humankind on his potter's wheel from clay. His symbol was a ram with horizontally twisting horns—the variety of ram's horn that Ogotemmeli said was symbolically the older of the two types. Two existing Egyptian hymns identify Khnum with at least ten other named deities, and H. W. F. Saggs suggested in *Civilization Before Greece and Rome* that such identities could extend even outside of the Egyptian religion. Khnum's cult center in Egypt was called Hermopolis by the Greeks; its Egyptian name was Khemenu, which means "the eight."

In the tradition of Heliopolis, the emergence of the first eight primeval gods and goddesses in male/female pairs seems to be in obvious agreement with the surface story line events of the Dogon creation story. The eight ancestors of the Dogon resemble the four pairs of gods in the Egyptian Ogdoad—Geb and Nut, Shu and Tefnut, Isis and Osiris, Seth and Nephthys. Egyptian sources are not consistent in the symbolism they assign to these eight gods, but modern sources seem to agree that the first four are meant to represent the classic cosmic forces—Earth, Water, Wind, and Fire. According to George Hart's *A Dictionary of Egyptian Gods and Goddesses,* Geb was the earth god, Nut represented the sky, Shu represented sunlight and air, and Tefnut was a goddess of moisture. However, based on linguistic similarities to other Egyptian hieroglyphic words, the name Nut seems most obviously related to other "nu" words like *nun,* which typically refer to water. The name Tefnut bears a similarity to Egyptian words beginning with "te," such as *tep,* which means "fire," and *teh,* which means "flame." Even among mainstream archeologists, Tefnut's link to water is considered a rather weak one, as Hart noted:

> Her connection with moisture is tenuously established from her position among deities representing cosmic elements and hints in inscriptions such as in the passage from the Pyramid Texts where the goddess creates pure water for the king's feet.[6]

As we have suggested, one possible reason for this confusion in meanings might be found in two separate passages from Dogon mythology. The first reference appears during a discussion of events surrounding the unformed universe, Amma's egg, prior to the "opening of Amma's eyes"—the Big Bang—in which the symbol of earth is counterposed with the symbol of sky. In *Atom: An Odyssey From the Big Bang to Life on Earth . . . and Beyond,* Lawrence M. Krauss described an equivalent scientific episode in the big bang theory, which took place at a point in the cooling process of the universe:

> After 300,000 years, the temperature of the universe evolved to close to the boiling point of iron. It now glowed uniformly white-hot . . . with every point glowing as bright as the sun. But there were not yet any vantage points from which to observe the sky. All there was was sky![7]

The second reference is found during the previously quoted discussion of the structure of matter, in which the four categories of quantum particles are assigned the symbolisms of earth, water, fire, and wind. Given the other resemblances between Dogon and Egyptian symbols, based on the Dogon pattern, it is possible that the confusion in the Egyptian symbols was the result of a blending over time of these two separate references, leaving us with symbols for earth, sky, air, and water instead of the expected earth, water, wind, and fire. Furthermore, we have already linked the Dogon symbol of fire to particles of matter and specifically to the symbol of the electron, which is a particle strongly affected by the electromagnetic force, which is in turn represented by the symbol for water. Because of the way these symbols relate to each other, it is easy to see how confusion between the symbolic references for fire and water might occur.

From a modern perspective, the belief systems of Heliopolis and Hermopolis might seem like separate theologies, but Stephen Quirke expresses the opinion in his book *Ancient Egyptian Religion* that based on the surviving Egyptian texts, the more likely case is that the symbolism of both cults originated as a single set dating from the earliest days of the Egyptian religion and that over time each cult center came to emphasize different aspects of the same original tradition.[8]

As we have discussed, many of the signature attributes of the female Nummo of the Dogon are apparent in the Egyptian mother goddess Neith, described by most sources as the earliest Egyptian deity and as the mother of the numberless Egyptian gods. She was sometimes called the first birthgiver—the mother who gave birth to the sun at the beginning of existence. In images she is usually shown wearing the crown of Lower Egypt and holding in her two hands a scepter and an ankh, the Egyptian sign of life. Neith, like the female Nummo, was a goddess of weaving and was said in Egyptian mythology to have woven the world with her shuttle. Perhaps originally a Libyan goddess, Neith's primary center of worship in Egypt was Sais, a city located in the Nile delta. In *A History of Ancient Egypt,* Nicholas Grimal tells of a temple founded by the first king of Egypt, Aha, and dedicated to Neith in honor of his wife, Neithhotep, whose name in the Egyptian language meant "may Neith be appeased." Inscribed on a wall of this temple were the words, "I am all that was, that is, or that will be." The Greek philosopher Plato identified Neith with the Greek goddess Athena, the patron goddess of Athens. Like the female Nummo of the Dogon, Athena's sacred animal was the serpent, and Greek mythology credited her with having taught the skills of agriculture to mankind. A later Greek myth in which Athena is portrayed giving dragon's teeth to Cadmus and Aeetes is closely linked to a similar Dogon story.

The first pivotal event in the surface story line of the Egyptian religion centers on the emergence of the god Amen, or Atum, from the primeval waters of Nun onto a mound of land called the primeval hill. In *A History of Ancient Egypt,* Grimal provided a careful description of this event that calls to mind parallel aspects of the surface story line of the Dogon:

There are three Egyptian cosmologies, but they all represent political variations on a single theme: the sun's creation of the universe from a liquid element. . . . The main system of cosmology was developed at Heliopolis, now a suburb of Cairo but once the ancient holy city where the pharaohs came to have their power consecrated. Not only was the Heliopolitan cosmology the earliest, but it also provided inspiration for Egyptian theologians throughout later periods of history.

The Heliopolitan cosmology described creation according to a scheme which is generally echoed by the other cosmologies. In the beginning was Nun, the uncontrolled liquid element, often translated as "chaos." Not a negative element in itself, Nun was simply an uncreated mass, without structure but containing within it the potential seeds of life.

It was from this chaos that the sun emerged. The origin of the sun itself was not known, for it was said to have "come into being out of itself." It appeared on a mound of earth covered in pure sand emerging from water, taking the form of a standing stone, the *benben.* This *benben* stone was the focus of a cult in the temple at Heliopolis, which was considered to be the original site of creation.[9]

Among later texts of the ancient religions of the world we can find many references that equate the first, self-created god, in various forms and names, to the sun. But C. Staniland Wake—a nineteenth century writer—tells us in his article "The Origin of Serpent Worship" that prior to the existence of this solar identity, these same gods were closely linked with the star Sirius in its aspect as the herald of the sun at the start of the planting season.[10] This observation by Wake is in complete agreement with the mythology of the Dogon.

The primeval hill, which the benben stone was said to represent, was originally conceived of as a kind of mound in a shape similar to that of Amma's egg and soon took on the form of a platform with stairs on each side, very much like the Dogon granary. In fact, the primeval hill was commonly represented by this Egyptian hieroglyph:

R. T. Rundle Clark wrote in *Myth and Symbol in Ancient Egypt* that the primeval hill is the concept that the step pyramid is meant to represent. We might recall that in Dogon mythology, the granary was an improved form of the simple mud hut, which took its shape after the pattern of the anthill. Clark suggests that the pyramid was the next logical step in a similar developmental progression in ancient Egypt. Saggs carried this thought a step further in a discussion of the primeval mound:

The mound of sand over a grave came to be thought of as magically equated with this primeval hill. . . . What Imhotep did was to transform the old mound of sand, encased in a stepped arrangement of bricks, into a massive structure which covered and enclosed the complete tomb. The pyramid was therefore to the Egyptians, a representation, or commemoration, of the primeval hill. This explanation does not depend upon theoretical deduction: the connection between the pyramid and the god Atum on the primeval hill is explicitly made in a text carved on a pyramid; by this identification the pyramid was linked to the origins and maintenance of all life.[11]

The benben stone—shaped like Amma's egg—held a place of importance and reverence in the ancient Egyptian religious traditions of Heliopolis that is comparable to that of Amma's egg in the Dogon religion. In Egyptian mythology, Ben is another name for the self-created god Amen. Like the icon of the god Min, the benben stone is described as a meteoric stone that was said to have been displayed in a place of public prominence at the top of a pillar or column of stone. The combination of the pillar and the benben stone came to be known as an obelisk, a fact that makes the relationship between the Egyptian gods Ben and Menu even more evident because an alternate form of the hieroglyphic word *menu* means "obelisk." The mastaba, an oblong burial structure with slanted sides, is understood to have been an intermediate step between the primeval mound or benben stone and the pyramid, as noted by Grimal:

> The *mastaba* reproduced, within the home of the dead, the primeval mound from which Atum created the world—and so stood as a symbol of creation. The texts also suggest [that] Imhotep decided to turn the *mastaba* into a square and to cover it with a pyramid. . . . The step pyramid method of ascension was, however, superseded after just over a century by the smooth-sided pyramid of the Fourth Dynasty. . . . The change to the smooth-sided pyramid and then the introduction of the *benben* [pointed capping] stone were intended to reconcile the conflict between Atum and Ra.[12]

The conflict to which Grimal refers, which brought about the transformation from flat-topped pyramids to the familiar peaked pyramids, calls to mind the previously noted discrepancy in the dimensions of the Dogon granary. One can easily imagine a theological dispute between those who felt compelled to follow the creation story description of a flat-topped pyramid and those who were devoted to the creation story mathematics, which described a peaked pyramid. The suggestion is that Imhotep resolved an impasse by adding the symbol of an unimpeachable religious icon, the benben stone, to the top of a flat-topped step pyramid—a move that would be comparable to adding a cross to the top of a church—and in the end satisfied both factions. Given what we know from the Dogon creation story about the mathematics of the granary, it is completely understandable that the largest surviving Egyptian step pyramid, built by King Zoser and located at Saqqara, consisted of six steps leading to a flat platform, because if we follow the creation story dimensions for the granary (discussed in chapter 5) and make the choice to incorporate the steps into the face of each side of a flat-topped platform, the mathematics of the structure automatically work out to six steps (see the diagram of the Dogon granary on page 62).

From a linguistic standpoint, there are clear connections between the design of Egyptian pyramids and the Dogon concept of the granary. The Egyptian hieroglyphic word for granary or warehouse is *ukher,* and the base of a pyramid is called *ukha theb-t.* As we recall from our previous summary of the Dogon creation story, the fire of the first smithy was established on the flat platform at the top of the granary. We also know that in some ancient cultures flat-topped pyramids were used as altars of sacrifice. So, given the parallels that we have already observed to exist between Dogon and Egyptian symbols, it comes as no surprise that the Egyptian word *ukha* means "fire altar." There is also ample linguistic evidence to associate the word *benben* with Amma's egg of the Dogon. There is an alternate form of the word *benben* that means "to hasten,"[13] which also defines the Dogon concept of Amma's efforts to begin, in a dynamic sense, the processes of the universe. This interpretation is wholly reinforced when we look to the word in the Egyptian language for "to begin," which is *shaa,* because *An Egyptian Hieroglyphic Dictionary* lists a second word with the same pronunciation that means "granary."[14] Moreover, the dual symbolism of the word *benben* as both Amma's egg and the granary is again supported when we look to the

Egyptian word *sehu*, which means "to collect, to gather," and "gathered into the store," as well as a second word clearly related to it, *sehu-t*, which means "egg."[15]

This relationship between the benben stone and Amma's egg makes it much easier to understand the otherwise obscure Egyptian symbol of the scarab. In Egyptian mythology, the scarab is known to represent the dung beetle, an insect that lays its eggs rolled up inside a ball of dung. This ball is an obvious natural counterpart to Amma's egg, which in similar fashion contained the coiled-up seeds of the unformed universe. Based on this identity, it is relatively easy to see how the dung beetle, or scarab, might have come to represent the creative force behind the egg.

After Amma's egg—the Dogon equivalent of the unformed universe—the first component in our discussion of the structure of matter was the atomlike po. If we search through Budge's hieroglyphic dictionary for words similar to *po*, we find an entry for the name of an Egyptian god Pau—a likely homonym for the Dogon word *po*. According to Budge, the name Pau might mean "he who is; he who exists; the self-existent." We can relate this word more specifically to the concept of an atom by looking to the related Egyptian word *pau-t*, which means "matter" or "substance." As mentioned earlier, the Dogon tell us that the word *po* comes from the same root as *polo*, which means "beginning," so it is not surprising that for the Egyptians, *pau* also means "primeval time," and *pauti taui* means "the beginning of time."

As we recall, the Dogon tell us that the sene seed—the apparent equivalent of electrons, protons, and neutrons—commingled at the center of the po, just as protons and neutrons commingle to form the nucleus of an atom. Hawking wrote in *A Brief History of Time* that protons and neutrons consist of known combinations of quarks. He stated, "A proton or a neutron is made up of three quarks. . . . [A] proton contains two up quarks and one down quark; a neutron contains two down quarks and one up. We can create particles made up of other quarks . . . but these all have a much greater mass and decay very rapidly into protons and neutrons."[16]

If we were looking for a sensible hieroglyph to represent either a proton or a neutron, we would expect it to somehow convey to us the idea of a particle created by the binding of three components. Furthermore, we would expect the Egyptian word to be linguistically related to the Dogon word "sene." Using these criteria as a basis for a search of the hieroglyphic dictionary, we easily find the word *sen,* meaning "they, them, their," and represented as the following hieroglyph:

An alternate reading of this hieroglyph might be "a particle [clay pot] is created by the binding [knotted rope] of three elements [the number three]." The related Dogon word, *sene,* seems also to refer to an electron because it is described as surrounding the po and making it visible by "crossing" in all directions to form a nest, just as actual electrons circle a nucleus. Again, if we were to imagine an ideal configuration of hieroglyphs for this word, we would expect it to include a reference to the electromagnetic force and to an electron orbit. In Egyptian hieroglyphs, the likely equivalent word for "nest" is *aunnu,* whose presumed root word is *aun,* which means "to open." Among the hieroglyphic characters that comprise the word *aun,* we find a most recognizable Egyptian counterpart to the Dogon diagram of an electron orbit joined with the symbol for water—the icon we previously associated with the electromagnetic force.

An alternate reading of this hieroglyph might be, "that which orbits due to the electromagnetic force."

We may recall that it was the sene seed as an electron that played the role of the $1/2$ spin particle in the Dogon story of the fire that was stolen from the Nummo. We suggested that the word "stolen" was a reference to the binding of two atoms via a shared electron to form a molecule. Based on this reading, we can interpret further connections between the Dogon word *sene* and the Egyptian word *sen,* which has two appropriate alternate meanings—one is "to bind" and the other is "thief," a meaning that clearly recalls the Dogon exclamation of "stolen."

The next aspect of Dogon symbols relating to atomic structure involves the four phases of the Dogon creative mindset: bummo, yala, tonu, and toy. We previously related these four phases to the four quantum forces—the gravitational force, the electromagnetic force, the strong nuclear force, and the weak nuclear force. In *Legends of the Egyptian Gods,* Budge provided an Egyptian example of this same mindset when he related the legend of the creation of the universe by the god Khepera:

> The story of the Creation is supposed to be told by the god Neb-er-tcher. . . . This name means the "Lord to the uttermost limit," and the character of the god suggests that the word "limit" refers to time and space, and that he was, in fact, the Everlasting God of the Universe. . . . Where and how Neb-er-tcher existed is not said, but it seems as if he was believed to have been an almighty and invisible power which filled all space. It seems also that a desire arose in him to create the world, and in order to do this he took upon himself the form of the god Khepera. . . . When this transformation . . . took place the heavens and the earth had not been created, but there seems to have existed a vast mass of water, or world-ocean, called Nu . . . and it must have been in this that the transformation took place. In this celestial ocean were the germs of all the living things which afterwards took form in heaven and on earth, but they existed in a state of inertness and helplessness. . . . Khepera gave being to himself by uttering his own name . . . and he made use

of words in providing himself with a place on which to stand. . . . [One] version [of the creation story] speaks of a heart-soul as assisting Khepera in his first creative acts; and we may assume that he thought out in his heart what manner of thing he wished to create, then by uttering its name caused his thought to take concrete form. This process of thinking out the existence of things is expressed in Egyptian by the words which mean "laying the foundation in the heart."

In arranging his thoughts and their visible forms Khepera was assisted by the goddess Maat, who is usually regarded as the goddess of law, order, and truth. . . . In this legend, however, she seems to play the part of Wisdom . . . for it was by Maat that he "laid the foundation."[17]

This Egyptian concept of "laying a foundation," which appears in the context of a myth that describes the creation of the matter of the universe, closely resembles the Dogon creative concepts of bummo, yala, tonu, and toy and is explained by means of the same architectural metaphor that is used in Dogon mythology. There are also linguistic links between Egyptian words and the Dogon concepts represented by bummo, yala, tonu, and toy. When we examine these associations, it is important to remember that in Egyptian hieroglyphic language, just as in that of ancient Hebrew, the vowel sounds were only implied and might well be as accurately represented by other vowel sounds. The hieroglyphic counterpart of the Dogon word *bummo*, which most closely represents the conceptual stage of a creative act, is *bu maa*, which means "truth," is a synonym for *maat*, and is based on the same root word, *maa*, which we said earlier means "to examine" or "to perceive"—a meaning that makes it a fair representation of the conceptual stage of an idea or project. The Dogon word *yala* is defined as "the laying of stones to mark the outline of a structure." Its hieroglyphic counterpart is *ahau*, which means "delimitation posts" or "boundaries." The third Dogon creative stage, *tonu*, is defined as "an approximation of the object to be created." Its Egyptian counterpart is *teni*, which means "to estimate." The final Dogon creational stage is called *toy*, or *toymu*, and is thought of as the finishing step in the creation of an object. The corresponding hieroglyphic word is *temau*, which means "complete," the same concept that is reflected in the name of the Egyptian god Atum, or Tum, whose name, according to Robert Graves's *New Larousse Encyclopedia of Mythology*, comes from a root that means "to be complete."

The phrase "laying a foundation in the heart" is expressed in the hieroglyphic language by the phrase *senti ta*. One meaning of the word *sen* is "to create," and the word *senti* means "to found" or "to establish." There is also a homonym for the word *ta*, which means "time." So, the spoken phrase *senti ta* could just as easily be used to express the concept "to create or establish time," which would be a perfectly appropriate act for a self-created god.

For the Dogon, the most fundamental component of the structure of matter was the thread woven by the spider of the sene, whose name was Dada. If we were to pursue the Dogon word *dada* in the Egyptian hieroglyphic language, we might first disregard what for the Egyptians would be the two implied "a" vowel sounds and focus instead on the two consonants. Ramses Seleem discussed this consonant sound in his recent translation of the *Egyptian Book of the Dead*. He wrote, "The Egyptian words for 'language' are *Ddt, Medu*, or *Ra-N-Kemit*. The root of the word *Ddt* is the verb *Dd*, which means 'to say,' 'speak,' or 'declare.' The utterance of sound is energy resonating in a spiral form, which is represented by the snake, the symbol of primordial energy."[18]

The previously cited passage from Budge tells us that speech, which is a symbol of the spiraling primordial energy, is precisely the tool by which the Egyptian god Khepera created the universe. By this correspondence, the Egyptian creative impulse and formative power of the universe equates conceptually and linguistically to the spiraling thread woven by the Dogon spider Dada.

All of this brings us back to Neith, the primeval goddess who was distinct from Amen and held no specific position in the surface story of the Egyptians yet was still considered to be the mother of all of the other Egyptian gods and goddesses and had no obvious counterpart in the Dogon religion. Based on our previous discussion, we recall that central symbols of Dogon mythology can be shown to represent each of the scientific building blocks of matter, starting with the atom, working down to electrons, protons, and neutrons, continuing on to quantum particles and quantum forces, and culminating in the string. The Dogon equate the four categories of quantum particles with the symbols of earth, water, fire, and wind and refer to the bottommost component —the string—as a thread. For both the Dogon religion and modern science, all matter is a by-product of the movement or vibration of primordial threads. When we look to Egyptian hieroglyphs, we find that the word for "thread" is *ntt-t* and the word for "weaving" is *ntt*—both from the same root as the word *net,* which is the Egyptian name for Neith. What this implies is that the true counterpart of Neith might well be the Dogon spider Dada, the weaver of the primordial thread. In fact, the connection between the Dogon spider and the Egyptian mother goddess is strengthened by an entry in the *Dictionnaire Dogon.* According to this dictionary, the Dogon word *dada* means "mother."

When Egyptian mythology states that Neith "wove the world on her shuttle," it is significant that this essentially attributes the existence of the world to the movement of threads—just like Dogon mythology and modern string theory. Moreover, the hieroglyphic language provides us with a direct connection to the coiled primordial thread of the Dogon by means of an alternate hieroglyphic word for "thread," *thes-t,* which comes from the root word *thes,* which carries two meanings: "to coil" and "to weave."[19]

Based on previous discussion, if the Egyptian word *ntt,* which means "to weave, to bind, to tie," were indeed to represent the scientific concept of the string, then we would expect the hieroglyphic characters that constitute the word to reflect some recognizable feature relating to the weaving of strings. In their book *The Matter Myth,* Paul Davies and John Gribben presented a series of diagrams that represent two types of intersection of strings.

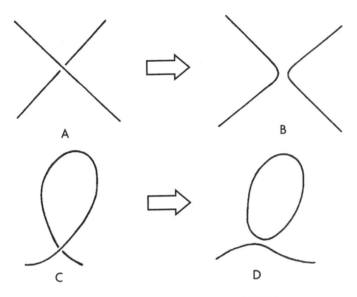

String intersections (from Davies and Gribben,
The Matter Myth, *186).*

The Egyptian hieroglyphic word *ntt* is written in a variety of ways. Two of the more common spellings of the word include as dominant characters symbols that precisely match the above diagrams and thereby reflect a relationship to the weaving of strings:

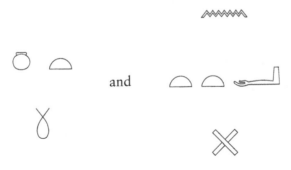

As mentioned above, the Egyptian name for the goddess Neith is Net, which can be written hieroglyphically in many different forms. We can only assume that if Neith in one of her aspects was meant to represent a string, then the hieroglyphic name of Neith would in some way reflect that scientific meaning. Compare the hieroglyph for Neith below with the corresponding diagram beneath it from Brian Greene's *The Elegant Universe,* which illustrates a more complex interaction of strings:

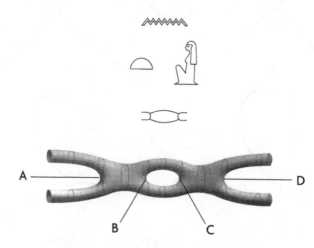

Complex interaction of strings (from Greene, The Elegant Universe, *292).*

We know that the first emergent gods of the Heliopolitan tradition were Geb, Nut, Shu, and Tefnut—the same gods that we previously showed were associated with earth, water, wind, and fire. With Neith as the mother goddess, we therefore have at the very foundation of the Egyptian religion the unmistakable symbol for a primordial thread who produces gods symbolizing the four categories of quantum particles, expressed in virtually the same terms as that of the Dogon. The sense in which Neith can be considered the mother of all the gods is the same sense in which the string can be considered the source of all matter. In support of this interpretation of the goddess Neith as a string, we find the following statement in an article by Katherine Griffis-Greenberg:

> Causing matter to exist and to live is the primary nature in Neith's primeval role in creation. That she does so without assistance of other deities is attested to her from the Pyramid Texts to the end of ancient Egyptian culture. Of all Egyptian gods and goddesses, Neith is often referred to in Egyptian texts as the "eldest," and even as the "first" deity. She is reputed, especially in the Late Period, to be the great creator of the world, and is often called by some

scholars the equivalent of the creator gods such as Atum and Ptah. As in the case of these primeval gods (though generally referred to as male), Neith is described in texts as either undifferentiated in gender or possessing both genders. As such, Neith should not be seen as [an] "original mother goddess" figure, as indicated in some references, but as an androgynous deity who creates the world from self-generation. However, unlike [those] gods who act after "emerging" from the void, the texts from all periods of Egyptian history indicate that she is, in fact, representation of the first conscious Act of Creation from the Void, who takes the inert potential of Nun and cause[s] creation to begin.[20]

We see that by means of myths and hieroglyphs, the Egyptian religion has succeeded in presenting clear definitions of strings, their purpose and structure, and the most common ways in which they interact using duplicates of not one but three highly recognizable scientific figures from string theory, all within the explicit context of a discussion of the structure of matter.

When Egyptian mythology speaks of Neith—our symbol for the string—creating matter from the "inert potential of Nun," we quickly realize that the root concept of *nun*—the celestial waters—must also have some significance related to quantum and atomic science. Again we look for an obvious hieroglyphic reference to define for us what aspect of science that might be. What we find are particles and waves, science's quintessential building blocks of matter, represented in the hieroglyphic spelling of the Egyptian word *nu:*

If we explore the Egyptian hieroglyphic symbols for "thread," we are also led to significant confirmation of a correlation with the idea of vibrating strings. The first of these comes from the word *set*, meaning "thread, string, cord," which is written by the combination of glyphs below, and the related word *sett*, which means "to tremble."

The association of these words also provides a clue as to why we find no entry in Budge's hieroglyphic dictionary for the phrase, "to vibrate." Apparently Budge chose to interpret the many Egyptian references to vibrations with a phrase of very similar meaning "to tremble."

The Egyptian hieroglyphic language also provides us with confirmation of M-theory, Calabi-Yau spaces, and the tearing of curved space. This confirmation is found when we trace the Egyptian words *pet* (spacious) and *peth* (to tear). It is interesting to note that the word *peth* bears a relationship to the name of the Egyptian god Pteh (or Ptah), who was defined by Budge as "the architect of heaven and earth." Compare the diagram from Brian Greene's *The Elegant Universe* directly below on the left, which represents the tearing of a Calabi-Yau space, with the Egyptian hieroglyph for the word "to tear" on the right.

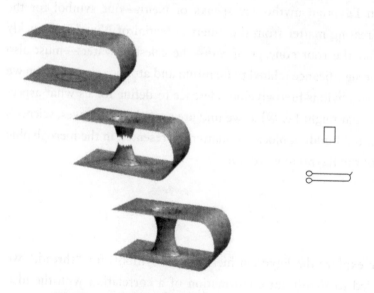

The tearing of Calabi-Yau
space (from Greene, Elegant
Universe, 264).

One of the ways in which the Egyptian hieroglyphic language expresses itself is by the use of determinatives—characters that are included among the glyphs of a word specifically to establish the context of the word. We find this same method at use among words that relate to scientific concepts. For instance, a character representing a hemisphere is commonly found in words relating to the structure of matter, and a character representing a square seems to be evident in words relating to concepts of space–time. There is a clear logic to these choices. The figure of a square seems like the quintessential diagram to define a space. Likewise, there is ample mythological precedent among the Dogon for the use of a figure of a hemisphere as a representation of the earth and the earth as a metaphor for matter.

The identification of Neith and the Ogdoad gods of Egyptian mythology with components of atomic structure presents us with an intriguing possibility—that there might well have been an intentional symbolic relationship between the original gods of the Heliopolitan tradition and scientific concepts relating to the Big Bang and the creation of matter. When we examine these symbols from this perspective and consider what we already have learned about the earliest Egyptian gods, a pattern begins to emerge. The gods Ben and Min—essentially two different names for the same god—are identified by the meteoric stone that in Dogon culture represents the unformed universe. Amen, the counterpart of the Dogon god Amma, represents the creative impulse by which the Big Bang was initiated—as the Dogon say, the very wind that scattered future matter to all corners of the universe. The Egyptian mother goddess Neith represents the weaver of the string—the fundamental source of the vibrations of matter. The Egyptian god Menu (also known as Min) is a composite of the four quantum forces—in a sense virtually a formula for matter. Strong support for this interpretation is found in the symbols of his hieroglyphic name, which take on new meaning when we look at the correlations between them and scientific concepts, as presented in the following chart:

SYMBOL	DOGON MEANING	SCIENTIFIC MEANING
℮	Spider's thread	String
⊙	Bummo (Earth/draw together)	Gravitational force (orbit)
∿∿∿	Yala (Water/bumpy)	Electromagnetic force
◯	Tonu (Fire/bows its head)	Weak nuclear force (particle)
⊓⊓⊓	Toy (Wind/drawing board or weaving loom)	Strong nuclear force (the atom)

This apparent correlation between the first Egyptian gods and aspects of quantum science presents us with what might be a valuable new tool for interpreting the symbols of the Egyptian religion. It implies that we might be able to segregate an original set of Egyptian gods and goddesses from later ones based on the degree to which the characters of their hieroglyphic names represent the properties of science they are understood to symbolize. Moreover, it provides a means for us to cross-check the validity of the scientific meanings we have proposed for Dogon symbols. Using this method, we are able to validate the scientific meanings of three key symbols by examining the hieroglyphic structure of the word *un*, which means "to be" or "to exist." (Not surprisingly, *unun* also means "to tremble" and "to do work in a field.") The glyphs for *un* simply and appropriately consist of the symbol for an electron orbit, the electromagnetic force, and the coiled string:

∿∿∿∿

℮

Some of the aspects of quantum theory that are most difficult to understand relate to the seeming paradoxes that occur when we examine the behavior of matter at the most fundamental levels. Richard Feynman says in *The Character of Physical Law* that the most important of these paradoxes can be demonstrated by a single experiment, which is conducted in three phases. Imagine that in a chamber we have a barrier with an opening in the center and a second barrier beyond that with two openings, each located a third of the way from either end of the chamber. Beyond the second barrier we have placed a detector that is capable of recording anything that passes beyond that barrier.

In the first phase of the experiment, we fire bullets in random directions through the single opening of the first barrier. Some of these pass through the two openings of the second barrier and are recorded by the detector. Because the bullets are fired one at a time, they do not interfere with each other and so create a specific type of identifiable pattern on the detector.

In the second phase of the experiment, we send waves of water through the single opening of the first barrier. Some of these pass through the two openings in the second barrier, and the intensity of the waves is recorded by the detector. In this case, the waves do interfere with each other, just as the waves caused by a passing boat will interfere with a nearby water-skier. Some of the waves cancel each other out, but other waves reinforce each other and so both create a different type of recognizable pattern on the detector.

Feynman says that when we try this same experiment using electrons instead of bullets, some unusual things happen. If we monitor the two openings in the second barrier and observe the electrons as they pass through, they form a pattern on the detector that is similar to the one created by bullets. In other words, the electrons behave as particles. However, if we do not monitor the electrons but simply record their arrival at the detector, they form a pattern that is similar to the one created by waves of water. What scientists infer from this is that electrons can behave like particles or like waves and that the act of observation somehow causes the difference in behavior. The method used in most cases to observe electrons is to shine a very bright light on them, which might lead us to believe that the presence of light causes the difference. In fact, the difference occurs regardless of the method used to detect the electrons. The more precise the method used for detecting the electrons, the more the pattern created is like that of particles.

This aspect of the behavior of electrons seems to be absolutely fundamental to the nature of matter, so if the Egyptian and Dogon creation myths are to be considered true examples of informed science, then it would be hard to imagine that the subject would not be discussed somewhere in these mythologies. Because the subject is so very basic to the workings of matter, the most obvious place to look for it would be near the beginning of the process of creation. What quantum experiments describe is an underlying aspect of matter that allows its smallest components to act as either waves or particles, with the change being dependent on the observation of an outside entity.

If we consider the details of the Heliopolitan creation tradition of Egypt that was discussed previously, what we recall is the description of an unformed, waterlike chaos called Nun. The god Khepera, with the aid of Maat—the god whom Egyptologists say represents truth or order—is able to speak a word (the Dogon say "weave a word") and thereby create physical aspects of the tangible world from the unrealized potential of Nun. We have previously talked about the Egyptian word *maat* and its root word, *maa*, and suggested, based on entries in *An Egyptian Hieroglyphic Dictionary* and *Dictionnaire Dogon*, that a more accurate translation *of maa* might be "to examine or to perceive." The name Khepera comes from a root that means "to transform." Based on these definitions, what the Egyptian self-created god Khepera has actually done is take the unrealized, waterlike potential of Nun and, simply by perceiving it, transmuted it into the primordial threads that form the words of matter. Both the Egyptians and the Dogon call this a process of "laying a foundation," and in fact, that is precisely what it is—the method by which the foundation of matter is laid.

To understand the phrase "laying a foundation in the heart," we need only explore the various Egyptian hieroglyphic words for "heart" and the words they sound like. One word for heart is *hat,* which can mean "the beginning" or "the frontier." In this context, we can see the process as that of laying a foundation at the beginning, or at the frontier, of matter. Another word for heart is *het,* which can also mean "the foremost part" or "the mind." In this context, the process might be equally well seen as one of laying a foundation for reality in the mind. An alternate meaning for *het* is "pot," our mythological symbol for a particle. In this sense, we see the phrase as a reference to "laying a foundation for particles."

We can see that what Egyptian mythology has expressed in the clearest of terms is Feynman's paradox of matter—that somehow what we call reality acts as a kind of filter to present the underlying version of matter in an ordered way. Egyptian mythology confirms this interpretation by using the word *maat,* one meaning of which is "order." The suggestion is that whenever this underlying reality goes unperceived, it behaves like waves; once it is perceived, it behaves like particles. This implies that what we call reality might actually be a translated or interpreted version of some other, more fundamental existence.

Because Egyptian mythology seems to describe this process, it only makes sense to explore the hieroglyphic words relating to it and see what more we can learn. What we soon find is that there is an alternate word for "thread," *nu-t,* which is written in hieroglyphs as:

The glyphs above include the symbols of a wavy line for water and the cutting edge of an adze, which means to "select, choose, or shape," followed by the symbols for a particle, a string, and the looped string intersection. The adze is the tool often carried by Amen in Egyptian art.

The scientific implication is that the act of observation somehow causes primordial threads to be shaved like planed wood. Likewise, we find many of these same glyphs in the Egyptian word *mu*, meaning "to look, to observe":

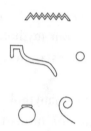

The quantum interaction by which waves are transformed into particles seems to be a critical one in which the act of perception makes an unrealized potential real, so it also makes sense to examine the Egyptian word for "real." When we search for this word in the hieroglyphic dictionary, what we find—appropriately and quite remarkably—is that the Egyptian word for "real" is *maa*.

The quantum paradox of waves and particles and their relationship to corresponding concepts in the Egyptian religion prepare us at last to understand the name of the Egyptian god Amen, known as "the hidden one," who is the counterpart to the Dogon god Amma. His name includes the following three glyphs, which we have not yet encountered in our study and whose meanings are taken from *An Egyptian Hieroglyphic Dictionary*:

    meaning "place or sanctuary"

    meaning "to hide or to be hidden"

    meaning "to interfere"

The name of *Amen* is written:

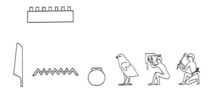

A literal and most understandable reading of the name of Amen might be, "that which draws or weaves waves into particles in a place hidden from interference."

EIGHT

DOGON PARALLELS TO GENETICS AND SEXUAL REPRODUCTION

The more we grow familiar with the Dogon creation story and its symbols, the more obvious it becomes that the correlations with fact extend beyond just the science of astrophysics. Indeed, one of the more remarkable aspects of the Dogon creation story is the way in which it seems to have incorporated three separate creational subplots into the context of a single mythological narrative. As mentioned previously, the first of these subplots tells the story of the Big Bang and the creation of matter—a theme that is altogether appropriate for a creation myth. The second subplot focuses on an equally appropriate creation topic— the story of genetics and sexual reproduction. We have already noticed obvious references to reproduction during our discussion of the surface story line of the Dogon. Even more remarkably, this second mythological subplot establishes itself by assigning an alternate set of meanings to the same basic symbols that defined the concepts of atomic and quantum structure. Like the story of the Big Bang, this subplot begins with the same initiating symbol—Amma's egg. In *The Pale Fox,* Griaule and Dieterlen provided a description and a diagram of Amma's egg as a symbol of reproduction. "Amma's egg is represented in the form of an

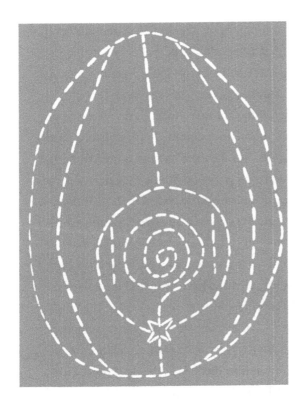

The second stage (yala) of Amma's Egg (from Griaule and Dieterlen, The Pale Fox, 118).

oblong picture covered with signs, called 'womb of all world signs,' the center of which is the umbilicus. . . . The oval contained the 266 'signs of Amma' *(amma bummo)*."[1]

On this alternate and symbolic level, Amma's egg represents a womb—the source of reproductive life—and at its center is a spiral containing the 266 potential seeds or signs. A spiral taken in the context of a womb can only call to mind the spiraling helix of DNA, which science tells us houses all of the seeds of potential that control reproductive growth. Looking at Amma's egg and its related mythological symbols from this perspective, we can again find many obvious Dogon and Egyptian references to support this alternate interpretation. The most obvious place to start is with the benben stone—the Egyptian counterpart to Amma's egg. Robert Bauval and Adrian Gilbert described the benben stone and what we know of its history in Egyptian culture in *The Orion Mystery:*

At Heliopolis there was an important sacred hill or mound upon which the First Sunrise had taken place, and belief has it that the sacred pillar stood on this holy mound prior to the Pyramid Age. At the beginning of the Pyramid Age, another, even more sacred relic either replaced the sacred pillar or, more likely, was placed upon it. This was the Benben, a mysterious conical stone which . . . was credited with cosmic origins. The Benben Stone was housed in the Temple of the Phoenix and was symbolic of this legendary cosmic bird of regeneration, rebirth and calendric cycles. In Ancient Egyptian art the phoenix was usually depicted as a grey heron, perhaps because of the heron's migratory habits; it was believed that the phoenix came to Heliopolis to mark important cycles and the birth of a new age. Its first coming seems to have produced the cult of the Benben Stone, probably considered the divine "seed" of the prodigal cosmic bird. This idea . . . is evident from the root word *ben* or *benben* which can mean human sperm, human ejaculation or the seeding of a womb. The mysterious Benben Stone disappeared long before Herodotus visited Egypt but not before it had bequeathed its name to the apex stone or pyramidion usually placed on top of pyramids and, later, the head of an obelisk.[2]

Bauval and Gilbert describe the benben stone as a womb, as Amma's egg also has been described, and cite reproductive meanings as the root of the word *benben*. We recall that the dual symbolism of Amma's egg was previously established by its relationship to the Dogon granary and to the Egyptian word *sehu,* which means "to collect, to gather" and "gathered into the store," as well as to the related word *sehu-t,* which means "egg." In fact, throughout history the very term *egg* has often been used as a kind of defining metaphor for reproduction and rebirth. Dogon symbolism related to the granary brings the idea of a womb directly into focus in another way because its external structure is thought to represent a woman lying on her back, with the doorway symbolizing her sexual part. From this point of view, the interior of the granary is well positioned to symbolize a womb.

The Dogon tell us that the spiral at the center of the womb contains the 266 seeds of reproductive potential. If, as we said, the spiral reminds us of DNA, then the 266 seeds would naturally make us think of genes—the component building blocks of DNA—and the chromosomes in which they are contained. This suggests that if we want to understand these symbols, our best approach might be to review what we know about chromosomes.

Every human cell includes twenty-three pairs of chromosomes, one of which is responsible for establishing the sex of the individual. Modern science groups the first twenty-two pairs of chromosomes together and calls them autosomes, but it is the structure of the final pair of chromosomes that ultimately determines which sex a person will be. These sex-determining chromosomes are shaped either like an X, with four branches, or like a Y, with three branches, and so they are called the X and Y chromosomes. During sexual reproduction, one X chromosome from the mother matches up with either an X or a Y chromosome from the father and thereby produces a female or a male child. In females, this twenty-third chromosome pair consists of two X chromosomes; in males, the pair consists of an X and a Y chromosome.

When discussing the twenty-three pairs of chromosomes, modern genetics makes a distinction between the twenty-two autosomes and the final pair of sex-determining chromosomes because this unique pair represents an exception to a rule that is worthy of separate discussion. Dogon mythology takes a similar approach when it organizes the 266 seeds or signs of Amma's egg. In *The Pale Fox*, Griaule and Dieterlen wrote about the organization of this spiral of signs within the womb:

> The sixty-six *yala* of the central spiral break down as follows: twenty-two at the center for the *po*, then forty for eight seeds, at the ratio of five per seed, and finally four for the *sene* at the tip of the spiral. The *po*, in the body of which Amma will build the world, is here understood to be the principle and prefiguration of the seed. . . . [I]t has twenty-two *yala*.
>
> At the center of the spiral of the twenty-two *yala* of the *po*, first

six *yala* are counted (as were the first six *bummo* in the breakdown of the picture of the signs). These six *yala* are the "sex of the po"; their number connotes the initial masculinity of the *po*'s sex, for three will represent, in man, the penis and the two testicles. The repetition of the number 3 underscores another fundamental aspect of Amma's second genesis: twinness. . . .

The six *yala* of the "sex of the *po*" are considered as the *yala* of the "sex" of the universe; they will also be the image of the sex of the first animate being formed in Amma's womb, the *nommo ana-gonno*, symbol of the human fetus.[3]

The Dogon description above compares favorably with the modern scientific understanding of the twenty-two human autosomes and the final sex-determining chromosome. The parallel nature of these descriptions provides us with a new basis for interpreting the Dogon numerological assignments of the number four as female and the number three as male because these numbers correspond to the X and Y chromosomes of science—the first, with four branches, produces a female child, and the second, with three branches, produces a male. Based on this interpretation, it is completely understandable that the number seven would then be numerologically assigned to the individual because it is the pairing of an X and a Y chromosome that determines the sex of an individual. Traces of this same system of numerology can be found in the following Egyptian hieroglyphs:

means "she," means "he",

 means "four" and means "seven"

During discussions of atomic and quantum structure in chapter 5, we found that the tribal drawings of the Dogon worked to reinforce the similarities between mythological descriptions of Dogon symbols and those from science. As we look at these same symbols from the perspective of sexual reproduction and genetics, we find that this is again the case. The identification of Dogon symbols with the science of genetics can be affirmed almost beyond dispute when we compare the scientific diagram below that relates to mitosis with the Dogon drawing of the yala of the egg of *nommo anagonno,* the first animate being formed in Amma's egg:

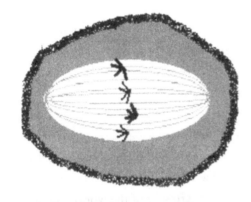

Chromosomes and spindles during mitosis.

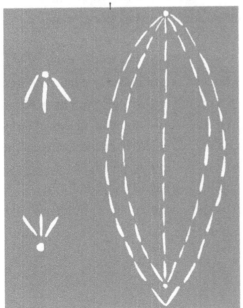

Yala of egg of nommo anagonno (from Griaule and Dieterlen, The Pale Fox, *160).*

Each of these two diagrams depicts a stage in the process of mitosis, which is a form of cell division in which the chromosomes duplicate themselves and spindles form that allow the two sets of chromosomes to move to opposite ends of the cell prior to its splitting. In *The Pale Fox*, Griaule and Dieterlen described the Dogon understanding of this same process in essentially scientific terms:

> [D]uring the division of the *yala*, the respective position of the *amma giru*, in relation to all those of the egg of the *nommo ana-gonno*, will play an essential role of orientation, as well as function as a sort of initial framework. Indeed, the *yala* of the four body *kikinu* placed themselves at the top of the egg (in the form of three strokes emerging from a central point) dominating it somewhat like the ribs of an umbrella. At the opposite end, the *yala* of the sex *kikinu* became inverted, placing themselves in the same way at the bottom of the egg.
>
> To emphasize the respective roles [the Dogon say], "the *yala* of the egg of *nommo anagonno* is stretched like the world that is going to spread itself out. . . . [T]he *yala* of the *nommo (anagonno)* caused the elongation (enlargement, growth) of the world." In fact the formed being will be complete and alive, therefore pure, and a promoter of general fertility.[4]

In the Egyptian language, we find an image similar to these diagrams of chromosomes and spindles in the prominent hieroglyphic character of the word *mes en* (perhaps a form of the word *sen*), which means "born of, brought forth by" and which is the single hieroglyphic character used to write the word *mesi*, which means "to bear, to give birth to, to produce, to fashion." The same symbol (seen below) is prominently used in the words *messiu*, which means "those who are born, children," and *mes*, which means "to weave, to spin."

Looking further in the Egyptian language, we find another similar word, *sen,* which means "to copy, to make a likeness of anything." Another word, a homonym for the word *sen,* has the meaning of "clay"—the very substance from which humankind was said to have been created.

If we accept for a moment that there could be a legitimate relationship between these symbols from the deep story line of the Dogon and the components of genetic science, then we might be able to use that understanding to identify mythological symbols from other storylines that are not well understood. An example of this is found when we consider the Anunnaki, or Anunnaku, the mysterious ancestral gods of the Sumerians. Robert K. G. Temple described the Anunnaki in his book *The Sirius Mystery:*

No certain identification of any important Sumerian god with any one of the Anunnaki exists except peripherally. . . . In fact, all Sumerologists have been puzzled by the Anunnaki. They have not been "identified" and no one knows exactly what is meant by them. They recur often throughout the texts, which makes it all the more annoying that nowhere are they explicitly explained. But their apparent importance to the Sumerians cannot be questioned.[5]

Needless to say, none of these seven Anunnaki is ever identified as an individual god. . . . No Sumerologist has satisfactorily explained all this. It is terribly imprecise and confusing—unless one had a structure to supply which fits under the cloth and matches the contours and thereby be accepted as a tentative basis of explanation.[6]

Other researchers agree about the lack of definition that surrounds the Anunnaki. In their book *Gods, Demons and Symbols of Ancient Mesopotamia,* Jeremy Black and Anthony Green touched briefly on the Anunnaki and defined them—as best as is possible—in the following terms:

The Anuna (Anunnakku), which possibly means "princely offspring," is used in the earlier, especially Sumerian, texts as a general
word for the gods, in particular the early gods who were born first
and were not differentiated with individual names.[7]

In the Sumerian culture, the Anunnaki hold a place that is parallel to
that of the eight ancestors of the Dogon, who were the predecessors of
the eighty descendants of the eight Dogon families. Ancient and modern
sources vary regarding the exact number of Anunnaki. For instance, in
the *Enuma Elish*—the Mesopotamian myth of creation—they are represented as the seven judges of the underworld, although other sources
cite their number as fifty. This variance in number from seven to fifty
might betray an original, underlying story similar to that of the Dogon,
in which eight original ancestors, one of whom was killed, later begat
eighty. Based on the genetic meanings associated with the deep story line
symbols of the Dogon and the identification of the eight ancestors of the
surface story line with germ cells, it seems reasonable to infer that the
Anunnaki are also meant to represent germ cells, which are created during the process of cell division called meiosis.

The Dogon symbol of the eight *kikinu* (shown earlier in this chapter in the figure of the yala of the egg of the nommo anagonno), which
are described in terms similar to chromosomes and drawn to look
like chromosomes, reinforces this same symbolism relating to ancestors and the number eight. Even the Sumerian term "Anunnaki," the
derivation of which we are told is uncertain, bears a resemblance to
the Dogon term *kikinu*. The separation of the kikinu into two groupings of four souls repeats the pattern of the two groups of four germ
cells, in a sense reinforcing their relationship with this aspect of sexual
reproduction.

Modern science has a clear understanding of how a fertilized egg
grows and develops into an embryo and then into a fetus. A sperm fertil-
izes an egg to create an embryo. Around the third week of an embryo's
development, a spinal cord and a brain emerge and a rudimentary heart
forms. By the fourth week the embryo begins to develop ears and eyes.

By the eighth or ninth week the embryo—now called a fetus—starts to form appendages. By the twelfth or thirteenth week the fetus begins to take on the appearance of a baby, complete with recognizable sex organs. In *The Pale Fox*, Griaule and Dieterlen related what the Dogon say about this same developmental process. Again, the tribe members seem to express themselves in distinctly scientific terms, even as regards the sequence of the stages in which an embryo develops:

> [I]n the first stage, the word in the *sosogu* was androgynous; it was the "life" of the being, still undifferentiated: it was "vegetative life." During the following stage, the "word" will be nourished by food, the essence of which will be passed into the blood. It will differentiate itself (into male or female), will take on its character by passing through the internal organs, beginning with the heart, which connects with the suprabranchial organs, thus associating the being's physiology with its psychology. The eighth articulation of the word will be in the sex, the reproductive organ that will permit the adult to give birth to a new being.[8]

The final four yala of the sixty-six signs in the spiral of Amma's egg are explained by Griaule and Dieterlen from a genetic standpoint using the same concepts previously cited in our discussion of quantum structure to describe the four varieties of quarks:

> The four final *yala* are assigned to the *sene*, here called "testimony of the former world" . . . and of the first genesis. Their number emphasizes the presence in the new universe of the four elements, preserved by Amma with the *sene*, in the following order: water, fire, earth and air, the last being located at the tip of the spiral.[9]

The above symbols, which in the first Dogon story line represent the building blocks of matter, can be interpreted in the second story line as representing the building blocks of DNA, which itself is constructed from components called nucleotides. Every nucleotide is made up of a phosphate and one of four possible nitrogen bases: adenine, cytosine, guanine, or thymine.

We recall from our prior discussions of the 266 seeds of Amma that the Dogon subclassify these signs into groups using two different methods. By one method of calculation, the groupings of these seeds were reckoned as six, then twenty, then four times forty. The number of signs in these groupings calls to mind key numbers relating to DNA. Rush W. Dozier Jr. discussed the genetic code in his book *Codes of Evolution*:

> The genetic code, as we have seen, shapes all life on Earth. It consists of a four-letter alphabet made up of four different kinds of nucleotides. These nucleotides are the structural units that make up the DNA molecule. The sequence of nucleotides on the DNA molecule provides all the information needed to make a human being or any other organism. A word in this alphabet consists of a sequence of three nucleotides and is called a codon. Each codon-word stands for one of twenty different amino acids.[10]

The structure of DNA represents one of the ultimate spiraling coils of creation. It resembles a coil in the shape of a spiraling double helix. In *The Pale Fox*, Griaule and Dieterlen conveyed the creation of the Dogon equivalent of the double helix of DNA in familiar scientific terms. The references in this case are expressed in relation to the creation of heavenly bodies but, because of the dual plotlines of the Dogon creation story, one set of symbols applies to both the creation of the universe and to genetic reproduction:

> This expresses the duality of "Amma's egg" and of the universe in formation—both are 266—for it is said that, while unfolding themselves, the spinning *yala* became twins. The emergence of the *yala* from the spiral crossing the signs of the collateral directions of space prefigured the future creation of all the heavenly bodies.[11]

Once again, we can see that when we apply the most obvious of meanings—those consistent with the beliefs of the Dogon themselves—to each of the creation symbols associated with Amma's egg, what is revealed is specific and accurate information about the science of genetics. The information compares favorably to an encyclopedia article on genetics, touching on each of the same subject areas and even providing us with a similar diagram, so recognizable that it hardly requires interpretation. The discussion of symbols that relate to chromosomes agrees in many details with what science tells us, and the parallels between the X and Y chromosomes and the Dogon numerological symbols are so embarrassingly obvious that we can only wonder that it took us so long to notice them.

The dual symbolism of Amma's egg, which associates the primordial quantum forces of the Big Bang with the genetic forces of sexual reproduction, is based on a fundamental equivalence that has not gone unnoticed by modern science. Dozier explained the quantum code in *Codes of Evolution:*

> The quantum code is the most complex and profound model ever produced by the human mind. Its usefulness is unlimited. By grasping the nature of atoms and molecules, physics provided the basic insight into understanding the genetic and synaptic codes. For the genetic code is constructed out of special kinds of atoms and molecules in the cell, while the synaptic code is formed by atoms and molecules in the brain.[12]

He also discussed the roles of particles and forces in the Big Bang:

> All the particles and forces we see today evolved from the Big Bang. . . . [M]ost physicists believe that there was no distinction between particles and forces at the Big Bang. They all blended together into a unified, symmetrical whole.[13]

In chapter 2, we identified Ptah (or Pteh)—the Egyptian blacksmith, sculptor, and fashioner of man—as another name for Khnum and a likely counterpart to the Dogon male Nummo. As the ostensible creator of man, we might expect Ptah to be connected in some significant way to the Dogon symbolism of genetics and sexual reproduction. Once again, such a connection is found in the hieroglyphic characters that make up his name:

It takes no imagination at all to see the double helix of DNA as the prominent symbol of his name, suggesting again an almost formulaic relationship between the hieroglyphic characters of a name and the scientific concept represented by a god. What's more, it seems that the figure of the knotted rope turns up again and again in words relating to human reproduction, making it—like the hemisphere and the square—another likely determinative of scientific meaning in the hieroglyphic language.

NINE

ARCHAEOLOGY AND DOGON SYMBOLS

The preceding chapters have shown a consistent and surprisingly high degree of correlation between mythological symbols of the Dogon, Egyptian religions, and concepts of science. Although these proposed relationships might seem compelling, they hardly can be taken as credible fact unless we can show that they also are supported by evidence from the archaeological record. What these mythological symbols strongly imply is that the creation stories that have survived from various cultures around the world are, in large part, remnants of a single, carefully composed narrative that was meant to serve as both the foundation for an ongoing religious tradition and the structure for eventual scientific learning.

The place to begin an archaeological discussion is with the beliefs of the earliest mythologies. There is little question that the earliest texts and myths of the first civilizations almost uniformly state that the skills of civilization were taught to humanity. For instance, the Egyptians believed that Seshat (the female scribe) invented writing and that Thoth (god of writing and knowledge) taught it to the Egyptians.[1] Among the Greeks, Apollo was the god of healing and taught man medicine.[2] In China, the god Shen-nung was said to have created the plow and instructed mankind in the arts of agriculture.[3] Each culture in its own way ascribes the rise of civilization to the teachings of its own indigenous gods. The fantastic descriptions of the interventions by these all-powerful gods make such statements difficult to accept at face value, and so modern science has turned to more complex theories of psychology to explain their near-universal appearance around the globe. However, there are alternate yet reasonable ways to approach these same statements that might help us make better sense of the message these myths seem to convey.

When my wife was a little girl—perhaps four years old—she and her six-year-old brother were playing outside near their house. They lived near a construction site for a college dormitory, and the two children jumped down into the hole that had been excavated for the foundation of the new building. When it came time to leave, my wife realized that she would have to crawl back up the muddy embankment to get out, and she did not want to get her clean new dress dirty. Her older brother, being larger, was able to climb out, and when he realized her dilemma, he went to get help. However, during the brief time that he was gone, two college students happened to pass by the site, saw the little girl stuck down in the hole, and lifted her out onto dry ground. When my wife's brother returned he was naturally curious as to how she had been able to get out. She told him that Superman had flown down and rescued her from the hole.

Any adult who might have listened to the facts of this story as told by a four-year-old girl would have soon realized that Superman could not have flown down and rescued her from the hole. Yet they also would have been faced with the undeniable fact that she was out of the hole, safe and sound, still wearing her clean dress, and that she had made it out in a relatively short amount of time. After a little consideration, the conflicting facts of the mystery would no doubt lead the adult to conclude that someone must have helped her out of the hole.

The rise of the Egyptian civilization presents us with a situation that is similar to the story of the girl and the hole. Credible researchers such as Nicholas Grimal and Sir E. A. Wallis Budge have expressed confusion at the very sudden rise of the Egyptian civilization against an archaeological backdrop that provides few precedents to account for its rise and little or no record of how it actually emerged. One commentator remarked that at 3500 BC, we find no hint of hieroglyphic writing, yet at 3400 BC, we find hieroglyphs in full bloom and in perfect form. A similar situation exists with each of the critical skills known to have been practiced soon after the emergence of the Egyptian civilization—agriculture, art, architecture, astronomy, and mathematics, to name a few. At 3500 BC, we find a tribal culture of hunters and gatherers with only the barest skills of agriculture, stuck in a kind of precivilized excavation hole. At 3400 BC, we see them standing proudly on the dry ground of civilization, telling us that Superman rescued them and showing precious few signs of mud on their dress.

Modern historians like Grimal have offered several competing theories for how this might have occurred. The prevailing school of thought simply postulates that a set of ideal conditions must have existed at that time to allow an unprecedented (and unrepeated) surge of growth to occur over a seemingly short span of time. During this period virtually all of the skills required for civilization were perfected simultaneously, and by some chance the archaeological record failed to retain evidence of that growth. A second school of thought, popularized by a modern group of often nonprofessional researchers called pyramidologists—led by researchers such as John Anthony West and Graham Hancock—suggests that the Egyptian culture must be a remnant of an earlier civilization, as yet undiscovered by modern archaeology. A third theory—first proposed by traditional scholars—states that a hypothetical third party—perhaps a dynastic race—migrated to the region at about that time and brought with it the rudimentary skills of civilization.

Each of these theories suffers from the same unavoidable flaw: because of the often sketchy archaeological evidence, none of them is supported by the archaeological record. What has not been carefully considered is the possibility that the very lack of an archaeological trail is itself evidence of what might actually have occurred, which is precisely what the mythological record consistently testifies did occur: a group of knowledgeable teachers came on the scene and deliberately helped to pull precivilized humanity out of the hole. If this was the case, then we would expect the archaeological record to show precisely what it does show, particularly in Egypt: a dramatic, undocumented improvement in the technological skill level of society.

One key drawback to the theory that the skills of civilization were taught to humankind lies in the present inability to identify a credible group of people who could have acted as teachers. However, the lack of a definitive cause has rarely stood in the way of a theory that is meant to explain an observable effect. For example, scientists have long proposed that the magnetic poles of the earth periodically reverse themselves. This theory was based on the position of iron particles in lava flows, which tend to orient themselves to magnetic north. Global changes in the direction of the orientation of these iron particles lead to the conclusion that the magnetic pole had shifted, even though at the time that the theory was proposed, no credible geological mechanism could be suggested to account for it. The similarities between mythologies of different ancient cultures present us with this same kind of global effect, and we see culture after culture pointing to the same explicit cause—an organized and informed teacher.

Pretend for a moment that you live in a basement apartment with no windows to the outside. Imagine that as you leave your apartment in the morning to go out into the world, you pass by several other tenants of the same building—some of them coming into the building and some of them going out. You notice that the ones coming in have red cheeks and one of them says to you, "Can you believe this weather?" The ones preparing to go out are wearing winter hats on their heads and boots on their feet. In this circumstance, you don't need to see a thermometer or hear a weather report to know with some certainty that you are about to go out into the cold because you have the casual testimony of a random set of people, none of whom has a reason to lie to you about the state of the weather. Ancient myths and texts present us with a comparable situation. The people of these early cultures have no reason to lie to us about their origins, and virtually all of them are telling us the same thing—that the skills of civilization were taught to humanity. Again, Occam's razor would direct us to the simplest of explanations—that the people in these societies, who are in substantial agreement with each other, might in fact be telling us the truth.

During the past few decades there has been much controversy over apparent Dogon knowledge about the star system of Sirius, which was sparked by Robert K. G. Temple's book *The Sirius Mystery* and based in large part on Griaule and Dieterlen's article "A Sudanese Sirius System." Dogon priests profess to know about the dwarf star—which modern science calls Sirius B—that orbits the larger star Sirius A. They seem to know that the dwarf star is very small and exceedingly heavy as well as the orbital period of Sirius B around Sirius A, which is approximately fifty years. Early artifacts from Egyptian culture support the parallel relationship we have suggested between Dogon and Egyptian symbols and underscore the importance of the stars of Sirius in early Egyptian society. In *A History of Ancient Egypt,* Nicholas Grimal tells about a calendar that implies that the Egyptian agricultural cycle, much like that of the Dogon, was oriented to the stars of Sirius:

A single text from Djer's [Egypt's second king of the First Dynasty] reign has affected the whole chronology of the First Dynasty by raising the question of the type of calendar being used. This text is an ivory tablet on which there is said to be a representation of the dog-star Sirius in the guise of the goddess Sothis, who was depicted in the form of a seated cow bearing between her horns a young plant symbolizing the year. . . . This simple sign would seem to indicate that from the reign of Djer onwards the Egyptians had established a link between the heliacal rising [of Sirius] and the beginning of the year—in other words, they had invented the solar calendar.[4]

An even earlier artifact than the calendar from Djer's reign is the temple to Neith that was mentioned in chapter 2. Plutarch referred to this same structure as a temple to Isis, another name for Neith. He described Isis as an alternate name for the goddess Ceres—who served as a known symbol for the star Sirius. Based on this identification of Neith and Isis with Sirius, we are now in a position to explore what the Egyptian religion might have known about the star system of Sirius and whether that knowledge corresponds in any way to the scientific data said to be possessed by the Dogon.

In Egyptian mythology, the most obvious characteristic of Isis was that she was described as being in the constant company of a twin sister named Nephthys—much like the stars Sirius A and Sirius B. Isis was a goddess of light and birth, and Nephthys was thought to symbolize darkness and death. These attributes correlate well with the brightness of the star Sirius A and the relative darkness of Sirius B. Isis was said to represent things that are visible, and Nephthys was the symbol of things that are invisible—again in complete agreement with the facts of the Sirius star system. Viewed from Earth, Sirius A shines as the brightest of stars, but Sirius B—in the words of Temple—remains "totally invisible without the aid of a powerful telescope."[5] The Egyptians considered Nephthys to be the opposite of Isis in every respect. Isis stood for growth and vitality, Nephthys for diminution—an apparent reference to the small size of the dwarf star Sirius B. In the Egyptian language, the word *nephthys* was also used to describe the extreme limits of the land of Egypt, much as the orbit of Sirius B delineates the limits of its companion, Sirius A. In *The Egyptian Book of the Dead,* Nephthys is quoted as saying, "I go round about thee to protect thee. . . . [M]y strength shall be near thee forever." Again, this can be seen as a reference to the orbit and density of Sirius B.[6]

Looking to hieroglyphs, we find that we can easily link Isis and Nephthys to other Dogon concepts related to the stars of Sirius. The Egyptian word *tuau* means "star of the morning"—a recognizable reference to Sirius. Furthermore, the Egyptian word *taiu* represents the number fifty—the approximate orbital period of Sirius B around Sirius A. Another alternate name in the Egyptian language for Sirius is Sbait. Significantly, *sbaiu nu mu* means "stars of the waters." In this case, it is interesting to note that the suffix *nu mu* represents the concept of water, just as the Dogon word *nummo* means "water." Continuing through the list of Egyptian names for Isis and Nephthys, we find the name Aarti, defined as the "two uraeus goddesses Isis and Nephthys." This name is a variant on the word *aart,* which refers to a "snake goddess." Thus

we learn that the uraeus—the figure of the rearing serpent worn prominently by the Pharaoh—is meant to represent the stars of Sirius. This
same pair of snake goddesses—again specifically representative of Isis
and Nephthys—are also referred to by the term *aknuti,* which comes
from the same root as the name of the Pharaoh Akhnaton and the symbol for life, the *ankh.* The word *aakhut* and other phonetically similar
words are defined as "wise instructional folk," "a name for Sothis [Sir-
ius]," the "eye of Ra," and a "ram-headed god." Akeru is the name of
the "ancestor gods of Ra," and *akhabu* means "grain." Thus we see that
the meanings of these Egyptian words that are related to Sirius convey
concepts that are central to the Dogon creation story.

Another early artifact of Egyptian archaeology is the pyramid, which
we have previously associated with the Dogon granary. The Dogon tell
us that the granary was meant to embody basic geometric shapes such
as the circle and the square. The Great Pyramid has long been of interest
to mathematicians, both because of its shape and because of its dimensions. There have been many scholarly studies done related to the mathematics of the proportions of the Great Pyramid.[7] One of these studies
was conducted by Joseph B. Gill, who wrote about it in *The Great Pyramid Speaks:*

> The perfect combination of form and function was intentional.
> Instead of being just a medium containing a message, a repository
> of knowledge as would be a library building, behold a medium
> integrating the first phase of its message in its exterior dimensions
> and geometry. The language of perfection, universal and unchang-
> ing, is simply mathematical relationships. How fascinating to think
> of such unchanging relationships being used! Even the verbal and
> written language of mathematics changes, just as the sounds and
> writing of any language change. What this means is one plus one
> equals two, no matter how it is written or spoken.[8]

Gill's statement illustrates the general sense of symbolic import conveyed by the Great Pyramid and the impulse on the part of researchers to

find symbolic meaning in the units of measure employed in its design.

One common theory of mathematicians, derived from the proportions of the structure, is that the Great Pyramid represents the earth. In his book *Secrets of the Great Pyramid,* Peter Tompkins ascribed the discovery of the earth-related mathematical symbolism of the Great Pyramid in the mid-1800s to a London mathematician named John Taylor:

> A gifted mathematician and amateur astronomer, Taylor made models to scale of the Pyramid and began to analyze the results from a mathematician's point of view. . . . [He] discovered that if he divided the perimeter of the Pyramid by twice its height, it gave him a quotient of 3.144, remarkably close to the value of *Pi,* which is computed as 3.14159+. In other words, the height of the Pyramid appeared to be in relation to the perimeter of its base as the radius of a circle is to its circumference. This seemed to Taylor far too extraordinary to attribute to chance, and he deduced that the Pyramid might have been specifically intended by its builders to incorporate the incommensurable value of *Pi.* If so, this was a demonstration of the advanced knowledge of the builders. . . . Searching for a reason for such a *Pi* proportion in the Pyramid, Taylor concluded that the perimeter might have been intended to represent the circumference of the earth at the equator while the height represented the distance from the earth's center to the pole.[9]

This conclusion is in complete agreement with Dogon symbolism for the granary because the Dogon tell us that the circular base represents the sun and the circle at the center of the square flat top represents the moon. The granary, which lies between the "sun" and the "moon," could therefore easily represent the earth. Likewise, when the Dogon tell us that the structure of the walls and ceiling of the granary represent a reclining woman, they are restating their own symbolism, which had been previously assigned to the earth. In so doing, they establish in our mind an equivalency between the two symbols.

If we pursue the mathematical symbolism that links the granary and the pyramid, we quickly come to see that there is an underlying mathematical basis to the Dogon creation story itself. Looked at from the right perspective, the episodes and events that take place in the creation story can be seen as a kind of tutorial in mathematics. Some examples of this are:

- The assignment of numerological values within the myth can be seen as a basic exercise in counting from one to ten.
- The number seven, which the Dogon call the "number of the individual" because it includes the number of the male (three) and the number of the female (four), provides an example of addition.
- The story about the eighth ancestor, who descends to earth out of sequence and angers the seventh ancestor who is ultimately killed, demonstrates that numbers have a deliberate sequence and provides an example of subtraction.
- The myth tells us that the eight ancestors were the first of an extended family of eighty, which is an example of multiplication. The same example is repeated in another form during the discussion of the symbolism of the granary when we are told that the one-cubit measure of the rise and the one-cubit measure of the tread of each of the ten steps of four staircases totals 80 cubits. This might represent one of two more complex mathematical formulas:

$$(1+1) \times 10 \times 4 = 80, \text{ or } 2 \times 10 \times 4 = 80$$

- As the story continues, we are told about the distribution of the eight heavenly grains among the eight chambers of the granary. This is a clear example of simple division.
- The Dogon tell us that the structure of the granary presents the basic geometric shapes, which include a circular base that is 20 cubits in diameter and a square flat top that measures 8 cubits per side. From this information, we can show that the circumference of the circular base, which is 64 if we use a rounded value of 3.2 for pi, equals the area of the flat top, calculated as 8 x 8,

or 64 square feet. In these results, we find that the area of the flat top provides an example of the square of a number and that the matching values for the circumference of the circle and the area of the square illustrate the use of simple decimals and demonstrate knowledge of the value of pi.

- The key numbers presented by the myths—one, two, eight, and ten —are important values in both binary and decimal mathematics.

These examples appear in the logical sequence one might expect from a simple tutorial on mathematics and include illustrations of—and the creation storyteller's apparent knowledge of—all of the usual and expected mathematical functions. The interesting structure of the granary —which is generally pyramidal in shape, although round at the bottom and flat at the top—could easily provide numerous other examples of higher mathematical and geometric functions.

There are resemblances between the alignment of the Egyptian pyramids of Giza and the stars in the belt of Orion. We also know, based on the calendar from Djer's reign, that the dates of the Egyptian agricultural calendar were determined according to the rising of the star Sirius.[10] Robert Bauval's Orion correlation theory suggests that the three large pyramids at Giza are positioned to represent the stars of Orion's belt. For the Dogon, the four stars or star groups associated with the faces of the granary, along with Sirius, were used as markers for various phases of the agricultural season. In *The Pale Fox,* Griaule and Dieterlen described how, as these stars appeared on the horizon or passed the point of zenith in the sky, the Dogon knew to initiate the next agricultural step:

> The three stars of Orion's Belt, oriented east-west, respectively represent the *nommo die,* the *tityayne* and the sacrificed Nommo, i.e., the guardians of the spiritual principles of the cereal grains that are entrusted to them between the harvest and the following sowing season. These are the stars that are therefore associated with the safekeeping of the grain seeds.[11]

Related agricultural symbolism is found among the Dogon in regard to the stars of the Pleiades, as shown by the following excerpt from *The Pale Fox:*

Recalling the identity between the child and the seed, the symbolism of the Pleiades is comparable to that of the kidneys; these stars are associated with the sowing and the harvest. The figures representing the Pleiades—which are like a "pile of harvested millet"—have nine dots for the "eight grains and the seed of the calabash in the ninth." "The grouped stars (Pleiades) in the world are proof of the eight grains of Amma which he will give as food (to man)." For these stars represent the seeds that the Smith will bring from the sky to man for the first sowing. Just before the rainy season, the [Pleiades] are not visible. . . . Their rising announces the approaching winter season, and preparations are made for sowing. This is determined by the rising of the [Pleiades] on the horizon; one says . . . "the Pleiades appear right on time." The harvesting takes place when they are at their zenith at sunset.[12]

The idea that Egyptian symbols were used to represent mathematical concepts is one that has long been accepted by Egyptologists. An excellent example of this kind of symbolic relationship can be found in the Eye of Ra symbol, in which each of the component sections of the eye is known to represent a simple fraction:

The basic way in which the symbolism of the eye works is explained by Christian Jacq in *Fascinating Hieroglyphs.*

Each part of the eye is worth a fraction. For example, the eyebrow is worth 1/8, the pupil is worth 1/4, the front of the eye is worth 1/2.[13]

According to R. T. Rundle Clark in *Myth and Symbol in Ancient Egypt*, each of the six parts of the eye, which is also called the Wedjat, represents a fraction. The rear of the eye represents $1/16$, the coiling tail $1/3$, and the base $1/64$.

> It will be seen that if each part of the *Wedjat* represents a fraction
> of the descending geometric series $1/2$, $1/4$, $1/8$, etc., put together, they
> make $63/64$, i.e., they approximate to 1.[14]

We already know that the earliest hieroglyphs appeared in an already mature form and remained remarkably stable throughout the history of Egyptian culture and that mathematics was one of the earliest advanced skills to be seen in that culture. Hence, the most obvious conclusion is that this mathematical symbolism related to the Eye of Ra was a conceptual part of the original symbol. The purpose of the relationship between the symbol and the mathematical concept was either a mnemonic one to help a student remember fractions or an instructional one to teach fractions, or both. As we think about the development of Egyptian culture, it is hard to imagine that a new civilization for which written language was an emerging concept could have had the awareness, impulse, experience, or sophistication to create an image with this kind of complex symbolism attached. One needs only think of the English language to realize how haphazardly a language grows, left to its own natural evolution. On the other hand, it is quite easy to imagine a knowledgeable teacher deliberately creating a symbol of this kind.

TEN

JUDAISM
AND DOGON SYMBOLS

Similarities between Dogon rituals and symbols and those of Judaism are important to this study for three reasons. The first is that the ancient Jewish religion is considered to be roughly contemporaneous with ancient Egypt, so the existence of similar rituals among the Dogon argues for the likely longevity of the Dogon tradition. By the Jewish calendar, the Gregorian year 2006 is rendered as 5766, a difference of 3,760 years; this would place the start of the Jewish calendar relative to the Gregorian at around 3760 BC. The second is the possibility that details preserved within the Jewish tradition regarding rituals that are also observed by the Dogon could provide us with corroboration of important Dogon priestly definitions. The third is that, because the Dogon priests have provided us with coherent symbolic explanations for many Dogon traditions, there is the potential that these explanations could shed new light on similar Jewish practices. It is not our intention here to imply a direct lineage from Judaism to the Dogon but rather to show that key elements of what appear to be contemporaneous and analogous symbolic systems were understood in similar ways by the Dogon, the Egyptians, and those who practiced ancient Judaism.

What we will observe when we compare shared Dogon and Jewish rituals are links to ritual words, symbols, and numbers that are also recognizable within the traditions of ancient Egypt. We start with the celebration of a jubilee year—a concept defined in Judaism as a fiftieth year, that is, the year that immediately follows seven sabbatical years. (This equals forty-nine calendar years because each sabbatical year consists of seven calendar years.) The Dogon call the celebration of this fiftieth year the *sigui,* a word that is pronounced like the Egyptian word *skhai,* meaning "to celebrate a festival."[1]

For the Dogon, the symbolism of the jubilee year—the sigui—relates directly to the orbits of the binary stars of the Sirius star system. Griaule and Dieterlen tell us that the fifty-year cycle of the sigui is based on the period of orbit of the dwarf star Sirius B around the larger star Sirius A, which is approximately fifty years. For the Dogon, the complete cycle of this orbit defines the period of renewal that is celebrated by the sigui. This makes sense if you imagine, after the passing of fifty years, each of the stars of the Sirius system returning again to its original orbital starting point. Griaule and Dieterlen described this system of renewal in "A Sudanese Sirius System."

> Thus the Sirius system is associated with the practices of renovating people, and, consequently . . . with the ceremonies which celebrate the renovation of the world.
>
> The period of the orbit is counted double, that is, one hundred years, because the Siguis are convened in pairs of "twins," so as to insist on the basic principle of twin-ness. It is for this reason that the trajectory is called *munu,* from the root *monye* "to reunite," from which the word *muno* is derived, which is the title given to the dignitary who has celebrated (reunited) the two Siguis.[2]

Publicly, the Dogon state that their sigui is based on a sixty-year cycle, but in actual practice it is observed every fifty years. This difference between word and action is attributed to deliberate obfuscation on the part of the Dogon priests, as a way of disguising an important calculation of their religion.

Another ritual that is common to ancient Egypt, the Dogon, and ancient Judaism and therefore merits careful comparison is the practice of circumcision—the ritual cutting of the foreskin of a male child (or in some cultures, the cutting of the clitoris of a female child). Modern Judaism only provides a kind of generic explanation for this practice, saying that it constitutes a symbol of the covenant between God and the Jewish people. Leo Trepp, in *The Complete Book of Jewish Observance,* provided a typical explanation of this tradition:

> Among people that practiced circumcision, the rite was usually per-formed at puberty. As some psychologists have pointed out, this may have been done to demonstrate the father's and the tribe's power over the son. . . . [T]he son learned . . . that he was forever bound to them by an individual covenant. . . . The Jewish child, by contrast, is circumcised on the eighth day after birth. . . . The Jew-ish child enters the fold of Judaism at birth. He enters the covenant on the eighth day of his life. Through this rite, Abraham became party to the covenant. His son Ishmael was thirteen years old when the commandment was issued and obeyed. Isaac, born later, was circumcised on the eighth day.[3]

Although a deeper symbolic explanation might once have existed in the Jewish tradition, most modern discussions of Jewish circumcision provide little detail to explain the practice. The Dogon, however, do provide an explanation, and the symbolism is once again tied to the stars of Sirius. The Dogon relate the circular cut, which defines the act of cir-cumcision, to the trajectory of the orbit of the dwarf star Sirius B (which the Dogon call Digitaria) around its companion star Sirius A. Griaule and Dieterlen discussed the practice of circumcision as the Dogon know it in "A Sudanese Sirius System":

> A figure made out of millet pulp in the room with the dais in the house of the Hogon of Arou gives an idea of this trajectory, which is drawn horizontally; the oval (lengthwise diameter about 100 cm. = 40 in.) contains to the left a small circle, Sirius (S), above which another circle (DP) with its centre shows Digitaria in its closest

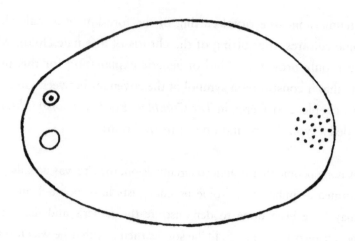

Orbit of Sirius B around Sirius A (from Temple, Sirius Mystery, *40).*

position. At the other end of the oval a small cluster of dots (DL) represent the star when it is farthest from Sirius. When Digitaria is close to Sirius, the latter becomes brighter; when it is at its most distant from Sirius, Digitaria gives off a twinkling effect, suggesting several stars to the observer.[4]

Griaule and Dieterlen explained the relationship of the Dogon figure above to the symbolic act of circumcision:

This trajectory symbolizes excision and circumcision, an operation which is represented by the closest and furthest passage of Digitaria to Sirius. The left part of the oval is the foreskin (or clitoris), the right part is the knife.[5]

We can learn more about the origins of the practice of circumcision by examining the history of its use in Egypt and Africa because it was practiced in both places. Herodotus, a Greek historian from the fifth century BC, makes specific reference to the practice of circumcision in his *Histories:*

The Cholchians, the Egyptians, and the Ethiopians are the only races which from ancient times have practiced circumcision. The Phoenicians and the Syrians of Palestine themselves admit that they adopted the practice from Egypt, and the Syrians who live near the rivers Thermodon and Parthenius learnt it only a short time ago from the Colchians. No other nations use circumcision, and all these are without doubt following the Egyptian lead. As between the Egyptians and the Ethiopians, I should not like to say which learned from the other, for the custom is evidently a very ancient one; but I have no doubt that all other nations adopted it as a result of their intercourse with Egypt, and in this belief I am strongly supported by the fact that Phoenicians, when they mix in Greek society, drop the Egyptian usage and allow their children to go uncircumcised.[6]

It becomes a simple matter to demonstrate a linguistic link between circumcision as the Egyptians practiced it and the Dogon symbolism that relates to the stars of Sirius. The Egyptian word *tuau* means "star of the morning"—a likely reference to the bright star of Sirius. A similar Egyptian name, Thaui, referred to the twin goddesses Isis and Nephthys. The Egyptian goddess Isis is known to represent the bright star of Sirius, or Sothis. Therefore it is reasonable to think that her twin, Nephthys, could also represent the dwarf star Sirius B. In Egypt, Tua was the name of the god of circumcision.[7] Finally, a similarly pronounced Egyptian word, *taiu*, represented the number fifty, which is the approximate orbital period of Sirius B around Sirius A.[8]

Another important link between the traditions of Judaism and the stars of Sirius, a link to Sirius that is similar to those of the Dogon and those that were confirmed by similar Egyptian references, can be established through a discussion of a traditional name for the self-created god of Judaism. This name, Ieue (or in Christianity, Yahweh) is derived from an anagram of the Hebrew letters *yud, hay, vav,* and *hay.* Based on previous discussions, we may recall that one of the hallmarks of the most ancient religions is that the letter representing the number ten (in Judaism, the letter *yud*)—also can be used as a name for God. The Hebrew letters of this anagram, which is considered an unspoken name of God, are the starting letters of the words of a Hebrew phrase meaning "I was, am, and will be," perhaps implying the concepts of past, present, and future. This phrase was loosely translated from an inscription found on the Egyptian temple to Neith at Sais, which was built by Aha, the first king of Egypt. In *Anacalypsis*, Godfrey Higgins rendered this inscription as it appeared on the wall of the temple:

> *I Isis am all that has*
> *been, that is or shall*
> *be; no mortal Man*
> *hath ever*
> *me un-*
> *vei-*
> *le-*
> *d*

In addition, Higgins wrote that a second text appeared on the same temple wall that explicitly established a connection between Neith and the stars of Sirius and between Sirius and the start of the calendar year in Egypt:

> On the front of the temple of Isis at Sais was this inscription, below that which I have given above: "The fruit which I have brought forth is the 'sun.' This Isis, Plutarch says, is the chaste Minerva, who, without fearing to lose her title of virgin, says she is the mother of the sun. This is the same virgin of the constellations whom, Eratosthenes says, the learned of Alexandria call Ceres or Isis, who opened the year and presided at the birth of the god Day."[9]

There are additional statements in the *Histories* of Herodotus that confirm a positive link between the Egyptian goddess names Isis, Neith, and Ceres (Sirius):

The Egyptians do not hold a single solemn assembly, but several in the course of a year. Of these the chief, which is better attended than any other, is held at the city of Babastis in honor of Diana. The next in importance is that which takes place in Busiris, a city situated in the very middle of the Delta; it is in honor of Isis, who is called in the Greek tongue Demiter (Ceres).[10]

Later in the same work, Herodotus discussed Apollo and Diana:

According to the Egyptians, Apollo and Diana are the children of Bacchus and Isis, while Latona is their nurse and their preserver. They call Apollo, in their language, Horus; Ceres they call Isis; Diana, Bubastis. From this Egyptian tradition, and from no other, it must be that Aeschylus, the son of Euphorion, took the idea, which is found in none of the earlier poets, of making Diana the daughter of Ceres.[11]

The Egyptian inscription corresponding to the Hebrew anagram of the letters *yud, hay, vav,* and *hay* seems to firmly link the self-created god of Judaism to the Egyptian goddess Neith. However, we have previously associated Neith, the Egyptian goddess who wove matter, with Dada, the weaver of the primordial thread in the Dogon tradition. This implies that the original underlying symbolism of the self-created god of Judaism might well have been in relation to the very same primordial thread. To support this suggestion, we would expect to find evidence that at the heart of the Judaic concept of God lies the notion of a primordial string as the source of matter. In *Anacalypsis,* Higgins provided us with precisely this evidence:

The similarity, or rather coincidence, of the Cabalistic, Alexandrian, and Oriental philosophy, will be sufficiently evinced by briefly stating the common tenets in which these different systems agreed; they are as follow: All things are derived by emanation from one principle: and this principle is God. From him a substantial power immediately proceeds, which is the image of God, and the source of all subsequent emanations. . . . Matter is nothing more than the most remote effect of the emanative energy of the Deity. The material world receives its form from the immediate agency of powers far beneath the First Source of being.[12]

Likewise, if part of the original symbolism of the god of Judaism was to a primordial thread, conceived in the same symbolic mode as that of the Dogon, then we would expect to find some reference in the cosmological traditions of Judaism to the primordial creation of the four categories of quantum particles: Earth, Water, Fire, and Wind. Such references can be found within the biblical story of Genesis and in the *Book of Jubilees*, which is a more detailed retelling of the story of Genesis, as stated by Willis Barnstone in his book *The Other Bible:*

> On the first day [God] created the tall heavens and the earth and waters and all the spirits who served him; the angels of the presence, the angels of the sanctification, the angels of the spirit of fire, the angels of the spirit of the winds.[13]

Even more to the point, there is a specific tradition within Judaism that assigns the symbolism of earth, water, wind, and fire to the letters *yud, hay, vav,* and *hay*—and most importantly, to the concept of the vibrations of matter. Marc-Alain Ouaknin wrote about the power of the name of God in *Symbols of Judaism:*

> When words, particularly those conveying the names of God, are inscribed upon physical objects of the world, these words send vibrations out into the physical world itself. . . . In Judaism, and in particular for the masters of the *kabbalah,* this life vibration is the name of God or the *Tetragrammaton*—the four Hebrew letters forming the biblical proper name of God, which often is inscribed upon physical matter.[14]

If we look to the creation story of Genesis in the Hebrew Torah as a likely source of other parallels between Dogon cosmology and Judaism, we notice that the events of the story line seem to embrace classic creation themes that are already familiar to us from previous discussion. In Judaism, the story of creation begins with a self-formed god whose spirit moves across the face of water to create light and darkness, then sky and earth. In much the same manner as the Dogon myths (and the other ancient myths they resemble) we can see within the story of Genesis an expression of the apparent mythological principles of twinness and the pairing of opposites. These thematic parallels, coupled with the common mythological symbols of Darkness, Light, Earth, and Sky, suggest an underlying cosmological basis for Judaism that it might share with the serpent religions found in other early cultures. According to Hyde Clarke, an eighteenth-century scholar, even within the traditions of Judaism we see strong historical connections to the concept of serpents as the bringers of knowledge.

Mr. [C. Staniland] Wake's hypothesis is somewhat more explicit. He is of the opinion that "Serpent-Worship, as a developed religious system, originated in Central Asia, the home of the great Scythic stock, from whom sprang all the civilized races of the historical period. These people are the *Adamites,* and their legendary ancestor was at one time regarded as the Great Serpent—his descendants being in a special sense serpent-worshippers."

But Adam, Mr. Wake suggests in another treatise, was not "the name given at first to this mythical father of the race." He suggests that the term was formed by the combination of the primitive Akkadian words AD, father, and DAM, mother. "It would thus," he remarks, "originally express a dual idea, agreeably to the statement in *Genesis* v. 2, that male and female were called 'Adam.' . . . When the dual idea expressed in the name was forgotten, Adam became the Great Father; the Great Mother receiving the name of Eve (Havvah), i.e., living or life"—(in Arabic, a serpent). . . . Mr. Wake gives the word *ak* the sense of "root or stem, lineage;" and so Ak-Ad [from which the name of the Akkadian civilization is derived] would mean the sons of Ad or Adam. . . . The Parsees of Hindustan have the legend of the great Ab-Ad, the first ancestor of mankind. . . . The Arabs also had their ancestor Ad. . . . The Egyptians, likewise, venerated a similar divine being, denominated At-um or At-mu, the Father of mankind.[15]

There are also hints in Judaism of two original creative beings, who are much like the Nummo pair, and an original pantheon of ancestor-like entities, who are similar to the Sumerian Anunnaki, the Egyptian Ogdoad, and the Dogon ancestors. Likely links to the idea of ancestral teachers come from frequent references within the Torah itself to *Elohim*—a plural Hebrew word that refers to gods rather than a singular god. George Foot Moore explained more about the concept of the Elohim in his multivolume book *Judaism in the First Centuries of the Christian Era*.

If the leaders of Palestinian Jewry had little fear of actual lapse into polytheism and idolatry, they had a greater concern about a defection from the strict monotheistic principle of a different kind, the currency of the belief that there are "two authorities" [or "two powers"]. The references to this error do not define it. A theory of "two authorities" might be entertained by thinkers who held that God is the author of good only, and that for the evil in the world another cause must be assumed; or by such as in their thinking so exalted God above the finite as to find it necessary to interpose between God and the world an inferior intermediate power as demiurge; or—as frequently happened—both these motives might concur.

The controversy . . . over the unity of the godhead . . . lies outside our purpose. It is sufficient to remark that the arguments employed on both sides are in large part the same as are found earlier in discussions of the "two powers." . . . [T]hey quote the texts of the Bible which most strongly affirm the soleness of God; and refute the inferences from the plural *elohim* ("God," not "gods").

That two powers gave the Law and two powers created the world was argued by some from the *elohim* in Exod. 20, 1 and Gen. 1, 1, taken as a numerical plural; to which the answer is given that in both cases the *verbs* of which *elohim* is the subject are in the singular number.[16]

Hints of an original Judaic pantheon, beginning with a single god but including two law-giving beings and a group of ancestor-like beings, corresponds to the Dogon creation story, which defines one monotheistic god (the one true god Amma), two intermediate agents of Amma (the Nummo pair), and eight Dogon instructing ancestors. From this perspective, each of the competing arguments within Judaism could be seen as true for the Dogon because, based on the Dogon pattern, it would have been quite possible to have two original law-giving beings and yet only one god. Godfrey Higgins, another nineteenth century author, addressed the issue of the multiplicity of names for the self-created god of Judaism in more detail in his epic work *Anacalypsis* and explained how this concept of many godlike entities might later have been transposed into the view of a single, monotheistic god:

But before I proceed, I must point out an example of very blameable disingenuousness in every translation of the Bible which I have seen. In the original, God is called by a variety of names, often the same as that which the Heathens gave to their Gods. To disguise this, the translators have availed themselves of a contrivance adopted by the Jews in rendering the Hebrew into Greek, which is to render the word *Ieue,* and several of the other names by which God is called in the Bible, by the word . . . Lord, which signifies one having authority, the sovereign. In this the Jews were justified by the commandment, which forbids the use of the name *Ieue.*[17]

Higgins also provided further explanation of the Jewish concept of multiple law-giving beings:

Perhaps there is not a word in any language about which more has been written than the word Aleim; or, as modern Jews corruptly call it, Elohim. . . . [T]he root of the word Aleim, as a verb, or in its verbal form, means to mediate, to interpose for protection, to preserve; and as a noun, a mediator, an interposer. . . . Jews have made out that God is called by upwards of thirty names in the Bible. . . . [T]he words *ieue-e-aleim* . . . mean *Ieue the preserver,* or the *self-existent preserver*—the word *Ieue,* as we shall afterward find, meaning self-existent. . . . Moses himself uses this word Elohim, with verbs and adjectives in the plural. . . . The 26th verse of the first chapter of Genesis completely establishes the plurality of the word Aleim . . . *and then said Aleim, we will make man in* OUR *image according to* OUR *likeness.* . . . From these different examples it is evident that the God of the Jews had several names, and that these were often the names of the Heathen Gods also. All this has a strong tendency to shew that the Jewish and Gentile systems were, at the bottom, the same. . . . It is a very common practice with the priests not always to translate a word, but sometimes to leave it in the original, and sometimes to translate it as it may suit their purpose. . . . Thus they use the *Messiah* or *Anointed* as they find it best serves their object.[18]

The four Hebrew letters *yud, hay, vav,* and *hay* act as a kind of bridge to yet another tradition shared commonly by both the Jews and the Dogon—the wearing of prayer shawls. We find a good description of the religious symbolism of the Jewish *tallis* in Trepp's *The Complete Book of Jewish Observance,* in which it is called a *tallit*:

A Tallit may be large or small. . . . A Tallit can be of any material, in any color; but it must meet two conditions: it must have four corners, and on each of these corners there must be a symbolic tassel, making four Tzitzit. . . . The Tzitzit must be white. They consist of four long strands, looped through a hole in the garment's corner and knotted. In antiquity, by command of Torah, one strand had to be hyacinth-blue. The white stood for purity; the blue for God's heaven. . . . Now we take the four strands of the Tzitzit; one of them will be very long, for it will be wrapped about the others. We put the four strands through the hole, seeing to it that, except for the long strand, they extend equally on both sides. Now we have a tassel of eight threads, seven of the same length and a longer one. We make a loop large enough for the corner of the garment to lie flat in it. This is done by a double knot. We now wrap the long strand *seven* times around the others and make a double knot with all of them. We must wrap the long strand *eight* times around the others and again make a double knot with all of them. Next we wrap the long strand *eleven* times around the others and make a double knot with all of them. Finally, we wrap the long strand *thirteen* times around the others and make a double knot with all of them.

Various explanations have been offered for the number of spirals. Adding the first three (7 + 8 + 11), we arrive at 26, a numerical value equivalent to the sum of the Hebrew letters in the name of God "YHVH" [*yud hay vav hay*]: 10 + 5 + 5 + 5 = 26. The Hebrew word *Ehad*—One—has the numerical value of the fourth spiral, 13: 1 + 8 + 4. The sum total of the spirals is, therefore, equivalent to the total in the words: *Adonai Ehad*, God is One. . . . The four corners may then call to mind that wherever we may be "in the four corners of the world," our task is clear.[19]

In Trepp's descriptions of the symbolism of the tallis, we find many of the key symbols of the Dogon religion. The four corners of the tallis repeat the symbolism of the four corners of Amma's egg, which represent the cardinal directions of the universe. The wrapping of the *tzitzit* in spirals repeats the Dogon symbol of spiraling coils. The double knot and the eight strands repeat the numbers of the Dogon creation story, two and eight.

Another Jewish tradition observed during morning prayer services is the wearing of *tefillin*—ritual boxes tied with leather straps to the arm and forehead of a Jewish congregant. Trepp mentions in *The Complete Book of Jewish Observance* that the reason for the rules relating to the making and wearing of *tefillin* were unknown to the rabbis. However, if we consider the use of the *tallis* and *tefillin* in Judaism in the context of the symbolic structure we have previously defined for Egyptian science, then these ritual practices fall into a neat and understandable package. We can see the *kepah*—a Hebrew skull cap—as the symbol of the hemisphere—a determinative based on a shape similar to the Dogon granary—to indicate that it symbolically represents the structure of matter. Likewise, the square tefillin boxes—symbolizing space—that are tied to the forehead and arm indicate the structure of space–time. The tallis represents the four cardinal points—that is, the four visible dimensions of space–time. The leather straps used to attach the box to the forehead are tied in a square knot, with the ends of the straps hanging down along either side of the torso. As a whole, these straps form the diagram of the "looped" string intersection. Likewise, the leather arm strap is wound seven times around the arm, once for each of the seven wrapped, unseen dimensions in string theory. It is then wrapped around the hand and looped around the fingers to form the Hebrew letter *shin,* which means "seven." In so doing, it has also formed an "X"—a diagram of the X type of string intersection. The fringes of the tallis are tied in loops and knots that resemble the shape of the complex string interaction and hang together to form a kind of membrane. The entire set of rituals appears in the context of a seven-day cycle, calling to mind the seven vibrating stages of a string, and are presented in front of and upon an altar called a *bimah*—which is pronounced similarly to the Dogon word *bummo* and the Egyptian *bu maa.* This altar mimics the shape of the Dogon granary and Amma's egg, which are symbols of the unformed universe, and includes an ark to house the Torah, which is in the form of a spiraling coil. During the course of the services, the ark is opened, the spiraled Torah comes out, and it is unrolled. Taken in this context, the prayer service of Judaism can be seen as a daily reenactment of the creation of the universe and of the structure of matter or, as the symbolism is expressed by Judaism itself, a reenactment of Genesis.

In *Symbols of Judaism,* Ouaknin noted that there is also clear evidence to connect Jewish symbols such as the tefillin to possible traditions in the religions of Africa.

> The ritual of the *tefillin* carries with it the idea of *zikaron,* memory and memorial. The four texts of the *tefillin* all express the idea of this "memorial" between the eyes. But the second text uses the mysterious word *Totafot* instead of *zikaron*—mysterious because it is not a Hebrew word. Rashi has ascertained that *Totafot* is a word . . . from Africa! *Tot* means "two" as does *fot* in an African language. Why is the word "memory" written in a foreign language, in this case in an African language?[20]

Another obvious similarity between the traditions of Judaism and the Dogon is found in the mythological concept of "the Word." In the Dogon tradition, each "word" is identified as a stage of instructional revelation that was provided by the Nummo to the Dogon. There are also several different tangible expressions in daily life of "the Word." The phrase can be seen as an expression of an actual spoken word, reflecting the notion of language as a key civilizing skill of society. It can be taken metaphorically as representing the concept of mass during the form of the completed Calabi-Yau space—the primordial "word" of matter. It can also be taken as representing DNA, a fundamental "word" of biology. Moore provided a clear explanation of the concept of "the Word" in *Judaism in the First Centuries of the Christian Era:*

> The fiats of God in the first chapter of Genesis are creative forces: "God said, Let there be light, and light came into being," and so throughout. "By the word of the Lord the heavens were made, and by the breath of his mouth all of their host" . . . (Psalm 33, 6, 9). The word of God is sometimes vividly personified . . . but it is an error to see in such personification an approach to personalization. Nowhere either in the Bible or in the extra-canonical literature of the Jews is the word of God a personal agent or on the way to

become such. . . . [T]he "word of God" in Hebrew scriptures is the medium or instrumentality of revelation of or communication with men.[21]

Moore's explanation of the concept of "the Word" contains many of the familiar elements of the Dogon myths, including the water-inspired connection between speech and breath, and the notion of "the word" as the instrument for conveyance of instructional concepts to man. As is typical of Dogon symbols that are linked with the mindset of bummo, yala, tonu, and toy, the symbol of "the Word" in Judaism is perceived by Moore as being somehow more than a concept but less than a fully personified entity.

Once we understand that we can correlate many of the central symbols of Judaism with those of the Dogon and the people of ancient Egypt, it becomes possible to use these correlations as a basis for understanding other central terms and concepts of Judaism. One such concept is the Judaic notion of an unspoken or unpronounceable name of god. This is the name that is written with the four familiar Hebrew letters *yud, hay, vav,* and *hay,* which for the Dogon might symbolize four fundamental stages or building blocks of matter. It is easy to see how the word *YHVH* could come to represent an unspoken name for god because it might never have been intended to represent an actual word in a spoken language. Rather, it seems to have been meant to stand for a conceptual "word" in the woven language of matter from which the universe is formed. Likewise, it is easy to see how the Hebrew word *adonai* could have come to serve as a spoken substitute for YHVH because in Hebrew, *adonai* means "universe." (This word might relate to the Dogon word *aduno,* which means "symbol.") In a similar fashion, the Judaic concept of a hidden name of god might be understood as a symbolic counterpart to the name of the Egyptian hidden god Amen. The twist might have been that Amen was called the "hidden name of god" because it meant "hidden." If so, the secret name seems to have been hidden in plain sight because it appears prominently at the end of every Hebrew prayer.

There are other similarities between the creation stories of Judaism and the Dogon religion that are worthy of note. Just as the Dogon egg of Amma contained the 266 signs or seeds or signs of creation, there also is a belief in Judaism that God's original creation included the twenty-two letters of the Hebrew alphabet—a belief that we recall is typical of the earliest religions. (In the Dogon mindset, signs are drawings that often take the same shape as Egyptian glyphs.) We may also recall that in the Dogon tradition there were certain religious concepts relating to the original creation of the po of which it was forbidden by certain classes of person to speak. Moore tells us that a similar prohibition is true of Judaism:

> Besides the public teaching of the school and synagogue, the first chapter of Genesis became the subject, or at least the starting point, of cosmogonic or cosmological speculations which were carefully guarded from publicity. The name for this esoteric doctrine was Ma'aseh Bereshit, "The Work of Creation," and in the Mishnah it is forbidden to expound it except privately to a single auditor. The restriction, which is made on the authority of Deut. 4, 32, does not apply to the exposition of what took place on the six days of creation, nor to what is within the expanse of heaven. But what was before the first creative day, or what is above, beneath, before, behind, it is forbidden to teach in public. . . . Against such speculations Sirach had given a warning which is quoted in the Talmud in this connection thus: "Do not inquire into what is beyond thine understanding, and do not investigate what is hidden from thee. Reflect on things that are permitted to thee; thou hast nothing to do with the study of mysteries."[22]

ELEVEN

THE DOGON
CONCEPT OF LIGHT

No discussion of the formation of the universe would be complete without consideration of the nature of light and its relationships to time and matter, and in this regard, the myths of Dogon cosmology are no exception. In fact, as we become more familiar with Dogon words and symbols, we come to realize that the concept of light resides at the very heart of key Dogon words and might often play the role of centerpiece in the Dogon symbolic system. To understand the importance of the concept of light to the Dogon and how it relates to science, it would help to first understand the nature of light as it is known to modern science.

In scientific terms, the speed of light (approximately 186,000 miles per second) represents the effective speed limit of the universe. According to Einstein's theory of relativity, this measured speed of light remains constant relative to all observers, no matter what their acceleration. This means that a person standing motionless in a field would measure the same speed of light relative to themselves as the pilot of a jet plane, moving at hundreds of miles an hour. Because, by definition, speed is calculated by the simple formula, speed = distance / time, then for the speed of light to remain constant in these two cases, the passage of time must slow down as a body accelerates. Stephen Hawking explained this concept in *A Brief History of Time*:

The fundamental postulate of the theory of relativity, as it was called, was that the laws of science should be the same for all freely moving observers, no matter what their speed. This was true for Newton's laws of motion, but now the idea was extended to include . . . the speed of light: all observers should measure the same speed of light, no matter how fast they are moving. This simple idea has some remarkable consequences. Perhaps the best known are the equivalence of mass and energy, summed up in Einstein's famous equation $E = mc^2$ (where E is energy, m is mass and c is the speed of light), and the law that nothing may travel faster than the speed of light. Because of the equivalence of energy and mass, the energy which an object has due to its motion will add to its mass. In other words, it will make it harder to increase its speed. This effect is only really significant for objects moving at speeds close to the speed of light. . . . As an object approaches the speed of light, its mass rises ever more quickly, so it takes more and more energy to speed it up further. It can in fact never reach the speed of light, because by then its mass would have become infinite. . . . Only light, or other waves that have no intrinsic mass, can move at the speed of light.[1]

From a scientific perspective, the emission of light is closely related to the way in which electrons orbit an atom. Science tells us that electrons are restricted to specific orbits around the nucleus of an atom, called orbitals and that an electron requires a specific amount of energy to remain in any given orbital. Lower orbitals require less energy than higher orbitals. For an electron to change orbitals, it needs to either acquire or release energy, usually as a result of collisions with other electrons. When an "excited" electron—one with more energy—loses energy and drops to a lower orbital, light can be emitted at a frequency determined by the amount of energy released. Because orbitals require specific amounts of energy, light is emitted in corresponding quantum units, or packets, that represent the difference in the energy levels required by the lower and higher orbitals. The form of light that we observe most frequently is called incandescent light, which is light whose energy comes from heat.

Astrophysicists tell us that the unformed universe—like a black hole—was so unimaginably dense that even light itself could not escape its gravitational pull. This means that, prior to the Big Bang, light did not exist—or as the ancient creation stories might say, the universe was "dark and without form." So, we can essentially think of light as having been created at the moment of the Big Bang. The Dogon creation myths are in agreement with the scientists on this point. They tell us that Amma's egg was formed prior to the existence of light and that it was the breaking of Amma's egg (sometimes called the opening of Amma's eyes)—the Dogon equivalent of the Big Bang—that was responsible for the creation of light. Because the concept of light is so intimately connected with the formation of the universe, we would expect to find recognizable statements within the Dogon creation myths referring to light and its basic properties as part of discussions of the formation of the universe. Once again, that is precisely what we find.

Passages that might pertain to light and its properties are found in chapter 2 of *The Pale Fox,* which is titled "Ogo." Ogo is the name of a mythological Dogon character who imagined himself to be the equal of Amma and aspired to create his own universe. The name Ogo calls to mind the Egyptian word *aakhu,* which means "light." According to Budge, Aakhu is also the name of the Egyptian light god.[2] Ogo also would seem to be an appropriate name for the symbolic Dogon counterpart to light because of its linguistic similarities to modern words pertaining to sight, such as the Spanish word for eye *(ojo)* and the German word for eyes *(augen).* For the purposes of this interpretation, Ogo should be considered to be the personified Dogon symbol for light, and we should view his actions as metaphors for the behavior of light.

As the Dogon describe him, Ogo has many different attributes that link him to the concept of light. Just as the scientific understanding of the emission of light is directly related to the "excitement" and movement of electrons, the Dogon statements about Ogo also begin by describing him as excitable, as being constantly in motion, and as being explicitly associated with the sene seed—the Dogon cosmological keyword we previously identified with electrons. As Griaule and Dieterlen write in *The Pale Fox:*

> Like his "twin" brothers, Ogo was attached to his formed placenta as a complete being. . . . But he was still alone. . . . Ogo demonstrated his anxiety and impatience. Although Amma wanted to form his female twin and give her to him, as he had done with his twin brothers, Ogo, in his anguish and desire to possess her, believed that she would not be given to him and he became incessantly restless. Thinking he was to be deprived of her, he "was irritating" Amma by moving about.
>
> Now, the lower part of Ogo's placenta was located in the same place where once the *sene* seed had been made. He wanted first of all to gain access to the first thing Amma had created and judged complete enough to entrust it with a creative mission. Ogo "touched" the *sene*, thinking he would find his own female twin in the place where the seed had been produced. But Amma had taken the creative function away from the *sene;* because of its failure it was now nothing more than a "germ."
>
> Nevertheless, Ogo tried to seize it, and he demonstrated his aggressiveness in that he himself did not want to be "touched" by the *sene* seed. They fought, and it is said that during this fight Ogo took away two of the *sene's* elements, water and fire, leaving it only air and earth.[3]

Metaphorically, we can see this passage as a discussion of the relationship between light and an electron. The episode itself touches on many of the key scientific attributes relating to light: the idea of light as being constantly in motion, the association of light with the attributes of an electron, and the idea that light is emitted by an electron after a change of energy level caused by collisions. From a scientific perspective, any reduction in the energy level of an electron is characterized by two effects: a change in the electromagnetically-induced orbit of the electron and the release of energy in the form of light. Mythologically, the Dogon counterparts to these collisions are described as fights that result in the loss of two elements by the sene: the mythological element of Water (represented in Egyptian language by a wavy line, which is the same symbol used in modern science to indicate the electromagnetic force) and Fire (a mythological symbol for light and energy).

Our experience so far with Dogon and Egyptian cosmological key words has led us to expect to find confirmation in the Egyptian language for important Dogon concepts. We have already correlated the Dogon symbol for the electron—the sene—with the Egyptian word *sen,* so if that correlation is a correct one, it would be reasonable to think we might find an Egyptian concept relating to the emission of light that is expressed by a related word. Once again, when we look to Budge's hieroglyphic dictionary, what we find is the word *senk,* meaning "rays of light."[4] Moreover, the word *senk* (displayed below) is written with hieroglyphic symbols that we have already associated with atomic science and electrons. An alternate reading of this word based on the concepts symbolized by its glyphs might be "the binding of an electromagnetic orbit releases thee," with "thee" referring to "rays of light."

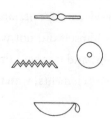

If our identification of Ogo as light is correct, then it makes sense that in one context his female twin as described in the Dogon myth must represent time. We know this because of the special link between light and time that is inherent in Einstein's theory of relativity. Hawking explained this relationship in *A Brief History of Time:*

> An equally remarkable consequence of relativity is the way it has revolutionized our ideas of space and time. In Newton's theory, if a

pulse of light is sent from one place to another, different observers would agree on the time that journey took (since time is absolute), but will not always agree on the distance the light has traveled (since space is not absolute). Since the speed of light is just the distance it has traveled divided by the time it has taken, different observers would measure different speed for the light. In relativity, on the other hand, all observers *must* agree on how fast light travels. They still, however, do not agree on the distance the light has traveled, so they must therefore now also disagree over the time it has taken. . . . In other words, the theory of relativity put an end to the idea of absolute time![5]

One consequence, as Hawking describes the theory of relativity, is that the faster one goes, the slower time passes. This means that no matter how fast or how long one travels, they can never "catch up" with the speed of light. In *The Pale Fox,* Griaule and Dieterlen related how the Dogon express this very same concept in relation to Ogo and his female twin, who represents time:

Ogo tore a [square] piece out of the placenta which contained his female twin in formation. . . . He thought he would be taking her with him by doing this. Amma, however, removing from the placenta the basic spiritual principle of being in gestation, put it out of his reach. . . . All Ogo's future attempts will be to look for and take back his lost female twin. . . . He will never find her again.[6]

The references in *The Pale Fox* to the piece of Amma's placenta taken by Ogo being a square lead us to assign the symbolic meaning of "space" to the shape of the square. This choice is supported by the appearance of the square glyph in various spellings of the Egyptian word *pet,* meaning "to be spacious."[7] Furthermore, Griaule and Dieterlen specifically assign Ogo primordial responsibility for the creation of dimension (space) and time—scientific concepts that are intimately related to the formation of light:

By his act, Ogo was the first to determine a series of sequences which prefigure, in their reality, both dimension . . . and time.[8]

Another key scientific property of light is its ability to be refracted into a spectrum of different frequencies. Refraction occurs as light passes through different media. If light hits the media at an angle, then several different frequencies of light can be produced, resulting in what we see as a rainbow. Any change in media has an effect on the frequency of the light, and therefore on the colors of visible light that we see. To describe this same phenomenon of light metaphorically, the Dogon tell about a mythical journey that Ogo took:

> Ogo started from the east, traveled towards the south, then went west and north in the opposite of Amma who, starting from the east, had begun the world in the north. Having thus begun his course in the opposite direction to the one followed by Amma, Ogo then turned in the same direction as Amma, thus completing a second path inside the first and tracing two lozenge contours, one inside the other. . . . These comings and goings "striped" his placenta as well as Ogo himself, who still bears the lines: three on the body and four on the face. . . . [T]he lines are as follows:
>
> body lines: red, white, black
> face lines: gray, yellow, green, blue.[9]

Although there are many different frequencies of radiation in the full electromagnetic spectrum, the human eye is only capable of seeing a portion of that spectrum, which we call visible light. In everyday usage, the term "light" refers only to the portion of the spectrum that people are able to perceive. In a similar fashion, Dogon mythology tells us that Ogo is meant to represent only the visible spectrum of light:

> Amma feared that Ogo might be able to make a world just as he himself was making one. . . . Irritated by this success, Amma cut off a part of his tongue, or more precisely, "the vein of his tongue." So

Ogo was deprived of the full pitch of his voice, thus of the range of sounds he was able to emit.[10]

The importance of light as a concept for the Dogon is underscored by the appearance of the word *ogo* as the central root in three important words: *hogon,* the title of the Dogon official charged with the religious enlightenment of the tribe; the name of the Dogon tribe itself; and the name of Ogotemmeli, the priest who was Griaule's instructor on Dogon mythology. According to North African ethnologist Helene Hagan, similar symbolic importance is placed on the root word *akh,* both in the Egyptian hieroglyphic language and in the language of the Amazigh, the hunter tribes that inhabited Egypt prior to the First Dynasty.[11] This root is related to important Egyptian words like *ankh* (the symbol of life), *aakhu* ("endowed with spirit"), *aakhut* ("wise instructional folk"), and *Aakhu-t* (a name for Isis, Sothis, or Sirius).[12]

TWELVE

GLOBAL SIGNS
OF THE SERPENT RELIGION

C lose study of the Dogon mythological tradition has given us an understanding and appreciation for its remarkable organizational design and for its many correspondences to Egyptian creation traditions. Perhaps equally impressive is the degree to which details of similar design are found in myths from virtually all corners of the ancient world. Recent archaeological discoveries now date the earliest appearances of civilized communities in the New World to approximately the same era as those in Mesopotamia and Egypt,[1] and there is little doubt that an organized society first appeared in China at about the same time. This kind of synchronicity in the rise of human civilization from continent to continent lends support to the notion of a common origin for the earliest mythological religions. Likewise, the existence of common mythological themes, symbols, and words among the earliest of these civilizations strongly supports this same suggestion. If we simply follow the familiar symbols and themes of the Dogon creation story as we know them, we will see that the same myths, icons, and idols form the basis of creation traditions from widely divergent regions of the world.

Just as the symbol of Amma's egg serves as the starting point for each of the themes of the Dogon creation myth, it also forms the basis of many other mythological traditions from India, Eastern Asia, and the Pacific Ocean islands. Symbolic parallels between the cultures of India and the Dogon range from a traditional Indian granary-like shrine called a stupa, which is built based on a symbolic plan much like that of the Dogon granary, to themes of Indian mythology, which recall familiar themes of the Dogon. These Indian themes were related by Arthur Cotterell and Rachel Storm in *The Ultimate Encyclopedia of Mythology:*

> Brahma, according to the Hindu mythology, was the creator and director of the universe. He was the father of gods and humans alike, and in classical Indian thought, he forms a trinity with *VISHNU* and *SHIVA*. . . . While the god Brahma meditated, he produced all the material elements of the universe and the concepts that enabled human beings to understand them. . . . [One] creation myth describes how, in the beginning, the universe was shrouded in darkness. Eventually, a seed floating in the cosmic ocean gave rise to a beautiful, shining egg. According to the sacred texts known as the *Laws of Manu*, "In this egg the blessed one remained a whole year, then of himself, by the effort of his thought only, he divided the egg in two." From the two halves, he made heaven, the celestial sphere, and earth, the material sphere. Between the two halves of the egg he placed the air, the eight cardinal points and the eternal abodes of the waters. . . . The egg finally revealed Brahma the god, who divided himself into two people, a male and a female. In due course, these two beings gave rise to the whole of the rest of creation.[2]

Although specific details of the Hindu creation tradition vary from the Dogon, the major themes are wholly apparent. First, an egg emerges from the waters of chaos. The name of the deity Manu, like others we have discussed, is a phonetic anagram of the Sumerian Nammu, which we correlate to the Dogon Nummo. The opening of the egg establishes the cardinal points of space and time and results in the creation of paired opposite entities. Finally, a man and a woman are created who become the ancestors of humankind.

Similarly, the elements of a somewhat different but familiar story line make up the basis of an East Asian creation tradition. Again, the following example is taken from Cotterell and Storm's *The Ultimate Encyclopedia of Mythology*:

> Myths of the creation of the world begin with emptiness, darkness, a floating, drifting lack of form or a fathomless expanse of water. Out of this dim swirl comes a more tangible object which holds the promise of both solid land and human life. The egg is a potent symbol of creation, and features in mythologies all over the world, including those of China and Southeast Asia. According to the folklore of the Iban in Borneo, the world began with two spirits floating like birds on the ocean, who created the earth and the sky from two eggs. In Sumatra, a primordial blue chicken, Manuk Manuk, laid three eggs, from which hatched the gods who created the world. A Chinese creation myth, which may have originated in Thailand, begins with the duality governing the universe—yin and yang—struggling within the cosmic egg until it splits, and the deity Pangu emerges.[3]

The East Asian myths repeat the classic themes of creation from water, the existence of a primordial cosmic egg, and the emergence of paired opposites. These suggest an underlying cosmological plan behind the different myths. Such details are pervasively echoed as far from India as Central and South America. We can see them expressed in various ways even within the Mayan creation story, which like that of the Dogon, includes three separate creational storylines (relating to the formation of the universe and of matter, and to biological reproduction), places emphasis on the importance of the four cardinal points, reflects the principle of paired sets of opposites, and assigns mythic symbolism to the concepts of Earth and Sky. Some examples of these themes were cited by Mary Miller and Karl Taube in *The Gods and Symbols of Ancient Mexico and the Maya*.

> The *Popol Vuh* has essentially three parts: first, the creation of the earth and its first inhabitants; second, the story of the Hero Twins

and their forebears; and third, the legendary history of the founding of the Quiche dynasties.[4]

The Mayan twin heroes, like the Nummo of the Dogon, are seen as celestial beings and are associated in some versions of the myth with Maize, a god of grains. Other similarities to Dogon myth are found in the traditions of the Aztec culture from Mesoamerica and South America, as seen in another example from Miller and Taube's book:

A widespread characteristic in ancient Aztec thought is the use of paired terms to refer metaphorically to a single concept. One of the best known examples of this is the Nahuatl term *alt-tlachinolli*. Composed of the terms for water *(atl)* and fire *(tlachinolli)*, this phrase refers to war, and the words for fire and water themselves are a pair of battling oppositions. In Aztec writing and art, this phrase is usually rendered as a pair of intertwined bands, one delineating fire, the other water.[5]

Yet another mythological theme of the serpent mythologies—the notion of the four cardinal points as pillars or posts upon which the world rested—is also reflected in the mythological traditions of Mesoamerica, as seen in the following passage, again taken from Miller and Taube's book:

Ancient Mesoamerican peoples widely believed that the cosmic balance of the world rested on the shoulders of four gods situated at the four quarters. For the ancient Maya, this skybearer was glyphically named as Pauahtun.[6]

The form and sequence in which the mythological gods of Mesoamerica emerged follows the familiar pattern described in the Dogon creation story. In one version, it begins with Ometeotl, a bisexual god whose name literally means "two god" and who was said to be the master of the "Place of Duality" in the form of two Nummo-like gods,

Ometecuhtli and Omecihuatl. This male/female pair, known in some regions as Oxomoco and Chipactonal, came to be the first ancestral couple and the progenitors of the human race.

For the Dogon, the first finished creation to emerge from mythological Big Bang at the opening of Amma's egg was the po, the symbol for the atom. The word *po* is linguistically similar to the name of the Mayan god Pauahtun, a resemblance that calls to mind the name of the Egyptian god of existence, Pau. Traces of the tradition of the po can be found in various early cultures, but none is more strikingly similar to the Dogon tradition than that of the Maori—a tribal people from New Zealand. In his 1963 book *Alpha: The Myths of Creation*, Charles H. Long described the importance of the word *po,* its meanings, and what it symbolized to the Maori:

> The origin of the primordial parents is understood to be the primal chaos in either the form of earth or of a watery chaos. Elsdon Best reports that the Maori have a word, *Po,* which has four interrelated definitions. These definitions are: 1) The period of time prior to the existence of the universe; 2) the period of labor of the earth-mother; 3) the period of time after death; and 4) the spirit world-underworld. This notion of *Po* among the Maori refers to the stuff out of which and the method by which creation comes into being. When the *Po* element is emphasized, the creation is seen as a gradual development from embryonic to mature forms in much the same manner as we saw in the emergence myths. The term *Po* in all of its connotations is a symbol of the earth mother who is before all things, who brings all things into being, nurtures them, and receives them at death. . . . One cosmogonic condition or phase resulted in another until they culminated in Earth and Sky, and one of the supernatural offspring of these primal parents became the progenitor of man. Inasmuch as all the foregoing offspring were of the male sex, woman had to be created from the body of Earth Mother ere man could be begotten.[7]

Other aspects of Maori cosmogony are also strikingly similar to that of the Dogon. An excellent source of material for comparison to the Dogon traditions is Elsdon Best's *Maori Religion and Mythology,* published in 1924:

[The Maori] taught his ideas of cosmogony by means of a singular allegorical myth showing the origin or growth of matter from chaos, or nothingness, and the gradual evolution of light from darkness. The superior version is to the effect that the Supreme Being brought the universe into being. . . . Two different aspects of all the superior class of myths were taught. One of these was . . . never disclosed to the bulk of the people, but retained by the higher grade of . . . experts or priests and by a few others. The other version was that imparted to the people at large, and this, as a rule, was of an inferior nature. . . . The former of these versions was that the universe was created by the Supreme Being. . . . A still more popular version, a fireside story, is connected with the origin of land, which . . . is said to have been hauled up by a god or demi-god from the ocean depths. . . . The earth and sky appeared from chaos or nothingness —that is, from the condition known to the Maori as the Po, usually rendered by us as "night" or "darkness," but which really implies the unknown. The origin of man is closely connected with cosmogony in Maori myth, for Earth and Sky were the progenitors of the race. . . . In any endeavor to obtain information concerning such matters as we are now discussing it is highly important that the inquirer should have access to the learned men of the community, the few who have been carefully trained in the tribal lore. This calls not only for a knowledge of the native tongue, but also for a long residence among them, ere the men of knowledge acquire sufficient confidence in an alien to induce them to impart such knowledge to him. The ordinary folk of any Maori community know but little of these "higher matters." . . . One can scarcely peruse any Maori myth or tradition without encountering references to the Po. . . . The origin of the primal parents Earth and Sky is often given, as we have noted, in the form of a genealogical table of descent from original chaos. As given by different tribes these differ considerably. Many of these lists of names commence with that of Te Kore. This word *kore* in the vernacular speech is a common negative form, the gerundial form *korenga* denoting non-existence. In Tregear's *Maori Comparative Dictionary* we find: "Kore: the primal power of the Cosmos, the void or negation; yet containing the potentiality of all things afterwards to come." These terms, then, the Po and the Kore, are the ones most often met with in descriptions of the conditions that existed prior to the appearance of the Earth Mother and the Sky Parent.[8]

Although the Dogon and Maori are separated by thousands of miles and immense expanses of ocean, the concept and context of the po is virtually the same in both cultures. The Maori confirm that the po represents a primary component of matter, which to them is the visible expression of the force of a mother goddess who gave birth to earth and sky. The coincidence of the term *po* being used in both cultures carries with it important implications. First, it shows that whatever influence might have resulted in its being communicated between the Dogon and the Maori could not have been a casual one, because along with the word and its symbolism we see a nearly intact transplantation of a complex religious tradition. Furthermore, according to both the Dogon and the Maori, the deep symbolism of the po was a secret tradition, which means that not just any sailor blown off course would have been able to carry it the thousands of miles of distance. Only a tribal elder—someone with privileged knowledge of the esoteric tradition—could have communicated it. The presence of the same tradition and its key symbols in two widespread cultures—both in distance and in time—serves as a kind of cross-check on the validity of both instances. It also adds support to the argument against a theory by Carl Sagan, which suggests that the Dogon adopted scientifically correct cosmological references to Sirius based on contacts from some modern-day visitor. Such a claim would require us to believe that the same modern information was transmitted to the Dogon and somehow also conveyed to the Maori at some point in time prior to 1924, which was when the Maori myth was documented by Elsdon Best.

We demonstrated in our discussion of Dogon and Egyptian cosmologies that the concept of the po as the image of the atom seems to have evolved from the same tradition as the concept of the primordial thread, which was woven in Dogon myths by a spider and in Egyptian myths by Neith, a goddess traditionally associated with Athena and spiders in Greece. According to Miller and Taube, the likely trail of this same symbolism also can be found in early Mayan mythology:

> In ancient Mesoamerica, spiders were commonly identified with female goddesses and the earth. At Teotihuacan, an important goddess . . . appears with spiders. It seems that this entity was considered to be a spider earth goddess, much like Spider Grandmother of the contemporary American Southwest. . . . In Classic and Postclassic Maya iconography, the old Pauahtun skybearer can appear wearing a spider's web.[9]

Miller and Taube also noted similar spider symbolism among the Aztecs at Teotihuacán:

> Although [the] term [Great Goddess] is widely used in recent literature, it probably subsumes a number of distinct goddesses. . . . Due to the appearance of spiders with this figure, she has been termed the Teotihuacan Spider Woman. . . . The significance of this goddess is still unknown.[10]

These apparent references to the po and the primordial thread are supported by their order of appearance and placement within the Mayan creation story and by their association with the mythological assignments of the cosmic elements earth and sky, which we have already associated with Earth, Water, Fire, and Wind. These examples identify the Mayan mythology as a likely relation of Dogon mythology.

One predominant symbol of these ancient religions—the serpent—

crosses virtually all known borders and boundaries and serves to tie divergent societies together. Students of ancient religions are no doubt familiar with the many forms that the serpent symbol has taken—from the rearing cobra in Egypt to the feathered serpent in Central and South America, the dragon in Eastern Asia, and the rattlesnake in North America. Hyde Clarke described the worldwide serpent image in *Serpent and Siva Worship and Mythology in Central America, Africa and Asia,* which was published in 1877.

> In every known country of the ancient world the serpent formed a prominent object of veneration, and made no inconsiderable figure in legendary and astronomical mythology. . . . No nations were so geographically remote, or so religiously discordant, but that one—and only one—superstitious characteristic was common to all; that the most civilized and the most barbarous bowed down with the same devotion to the same engrossing deity; and that this deity either *was* or was *represented by* the same sacred serpent. Its antiquity must be accredited to a period far antedating all history.[11]

The influence of the serpent symbol spanned a very wide set of regions, religions, and societies and was most commonly associated with the acquisition of wisdom. In time, the serpent came to be an almost standard symbol of kingship and authority. C. Staniland Wake described this symbolism in "The Origin of Serpent Worship":

> One of the best-known attributes of the serpent is WISDOM. The Hebrew tradition of the fall speaks of that animal as the most subtile of the beasts of the field; and the founder of Christianity tells his disciples to be as wise as serpents, though as harmless as doves. Among the ancients the serpent was consulted as an oracle, and Maury points out that it played an important part in the life of several celebrated Greek diviners. . . . The serpent was associated with Apollo and Athene, the Grecian deities of wisdom, as well as with the Egyptian Kneph (Warburton supposes that the worship of the

One God Kneph was changed into that of the dragon or winged-serpent Knuphis), the ram-headed god from whom the Gnostics are sometimes said to have derived their idea of the *Sophia*. This personification of divine wisdom is undoubtedly represented on Gnostic gems under the form of the serpent. In Hindoo mythology there is the same association between the animal and the idea of wisdom. Siva, as Sambhu, is the patron of the Brahmanic order, and, as shown by his being three-eyed, is essentially a god possessing high intellectual attributes. Vishnu also is a god of wisdom, but of the . . . type which is distinctive of the worshippers of truth under its feminine aspect. The connection between wisdom and the serpent is best seen, however, in the Hindu legends as to the Nagas. Mr. Fergusson remarks that "the Naga appears everywhere in the Vaishnava tradition. There is no more common representation of Vishnu than as reposing on the Sesha, the celestial seven-headed snake, contemplating the creation of the world. . . . The *Upanishads* refer to the science of the serpents, by which is meant the wisdom of the mysterious Nagas who, according to Buddhistic legend, reside under Mount Meru, and in the waters of the terrestrial world. One of the sacred books of the Tibetan Buddhists is fabled to have been received from the Nagas.[12]

Griaule himself noticed many commonalities between Dogon myths and the classical Greek myths. This is understandable because we have seen that ancient writers like Herodotus credited Egypt as the original source of many of the Greek mythological references. Such similarities are reflected in the retelling of the Greek story of creation by Edith Hamilton:

Long before the gods appeared, in the dim past, uncounted ages ago, there was only the formless confusion of Chaos brooded over by unbroken darkness. At last, but how no one ever tried to explain, two children were born to the shapeless nothingness. Night was the child of Chaos and so was Erebus, which is the unfathomable depth where death dwells. In the whole universe there was nothing else; all was black, empty, silent, endless.

And then a marvel of marvels came to pass. In some mysterious way, from this horror of blank boundless vacancy the best of all things came into being. A great playwright, the comic poet Aristophanes, describes its coming in words often quoted:

> . . . *Black winged Night*
> *Into the bosom of Erebus dark and deep*
> *Laid a wind-born egg, and as the seasons rolled*
> *Forth sprang Love, the longed-for, shining, with*
> *wings of gold.*

From darkness and from death Love was born, and with its birth, order and beauty began to banish blind confusion. Love created Light with its companion, radiant Day.

What took place next was the creation of the earth, but this, too, no one ever tried to explain. It just happened. With the coming of love and light it seemed natural that the earth also should appear. . . . Earth was the solid ground, yet vaguely a personality, too. Heaven was the blue vault on high, but it acted in some ways as a human being would. To the people who told these stories all the universe was alive with the same kind of life they knew in themselves. They were individual persons, so they personified everything which had the obvious marks of life, everything which moved and changed: earth in winter and summer; the sky with its shifting stars; the restless sea, and so on. It was only a dim personification; something vague and immense which with its motion brought about change and therefore was alive.[13]

Other recognizable details of the Dogon and Egyptian myths are apparent in a second Greek cosmological story line, as retold by Thomas Bulfinch:

There is another cosmogony, or account of the creation, according to which Earth, Erebus, and Love were the first of beings. Love (Eros) issued from the egg of Night, which floated on Chaos. By his arrows and torch he pierced and vivified all things, producing life and joy.

Saturn and Rhea were not the only Titans. There were others, whose names were Oceanus, Hyperion, Iapetus, and Ophion, males; and Themis, Mnemosyne, Euronome, females. They are spoken of as the elder gods, whose dominion was afterwards transferred to others. Saturn yielded to Jupiter, Oceanus to Neptune, Hyperion to Apollo. Hyperion was the father of the Sun, Moon and Dawn. He is therefore the original sun-god, and is painted with the splendor and beauty which were afterward bestowed on Apollo.[14]

We find that the symbol of the serpent is often expressed in ancient cultures in terms of the classic elements of mythology as previously discussed. In "The Origin of Serpent Worship," for instance, Wake, noted instances of symbolism associated with the letters of the alphabet:

The "serpent-science" of Hindu legend has a curious parallel in Phoenician mythology. The invention of the Phoenician written character is referred to the god Taaut or Thoth, whose snake-symbol bears his name Tet, and is used to represent the ninth letter of the alphabet *teth,* which in the oldest Phoenician character has the form of the snake curling itself up. Philo thus explains the form of the letter *theta,* and that the god from whom it took its name was designated by the Egyptians as a serpent curled up, with its head turned inwards. Philo adds that the letters of the Phoenician alphabet "are those formed by means of serpents; afterward, when they built temples they assigned them a place in the adytums, instituted various ceremonies and solemnities in honor of them, and adored them as the supreme gods, rulers of the universe." Bunsen thinks the sense of this passage is "that the forms and movements of serpents were employed in the invention of the oldest letters, which represent the gods." . . . According to another tradition, the ancient theology of Egypt was said to have been given by the Agathodaemon, who was the benefactor of all mankind. . . . Among various African tribes this animal is viewed with great veneration, under the belief that it is often the re-embodiment of a deceased ancestor. . . . Mr. Squier remarks that "many of the North American tribes entertain a superstitious regard for serpents.". . . Charlevoix states that the Natchez had the figure of a rattlesnake, carved from wood, placed among other objects upon the altar of their temple, to which they paid great honor. Heckwelder relates that the Linni Linape called the rattlesnake "grandfather" and would on no account allow it to be destroyed. . . . Carver also mentions an instance of similar regard on the part of a Menominee Indian, who carried a rattle-snake constantly with him, "treating it as a deity, and calling it his great father." . . . The most curious notion, however, is that of the Mexicans, who always represented the first woman, whose name was translated by the old Spanish writers "the woman of our flesh," as accompanied by a great male serpent. This serpent is the sun-god *Tonacatl-coatl,* the principal deity of the Mexican pan-theon, and his female companion, the goddess mother of mankind, has the title *cihua-cohuatl,* which signifies "woman of the serpent." With the Peruvians, also, the principal deity was the serpent-sun, whose wife, the female serpent, gave birth to a boy and a girl from whom all mankind were said to be descended. It is remarkable that the serpent-origin thus ascribed to the human race is not confined to the aborigines of America. According to Herodotus, the primeval mother of the Scyths was a monster, half woman and half serpent. This reminds us of the serpent-parentage ascribed to various per-sonages of classical antiquity.[15]

It is obvious from the above passages that the serpent symbol alone provides a common and compelling link among many of the oldest reli-gions from many different regions of the world. This link becomes even more obvious if we include among our serpent symbols the traditional dragons of Eastern Asia. We can find many familiar Dogon symbols in the following entry on Chinese dragons from *The Ultimate Encyclopedia of Mythology*:

The Chinese Dragon came first in the mythical hierarchy of 360 scaly creatures, and was one of the four animals who symbolized the cardinal points. Associated with the east, the dragon stood for sunrise, spring and fertility and was opposed by the white tiger of the west, who represented death. Daoist dragons were benevolent spirits associated with happiness and prosperity, and were kind to humans. However, when Buddhism became popular, their character was modified by the Indian concept of the naga, which was a more menacing creature. In folk religion, the Long Wang were dragon kings who had authority over life and death because they were responsible for rain, without which life could not continue, and funerals. They were gods of wisdom, strength and goodness.[16]

Likewise, Mayan symbolism of the serpent falls into almost direct accord with that of familiar Dogon mythology. It echoes many of the basic Dogon notions about the serpent symbol and its relationship to water and spiraling coils, as Miller and Taube noted:

In religious terms, serpents may have been the most important fauna of Mesoamerica. No single other type of creature receives such elaborate treatment in Sahagun's Florentine Codex. . . . Three fundamental notions accompany the Mesoamerican serpent: one, that the serpent is water, the conduit of water, or the bearer of water; two, that its mouth opens to a cave; and three, that the serpent is the sky. . . . Mesoamerican people believed in serpent deities from earliest times.[17]

Why the serpent, of all possible creatures, should so thoroughly dominate the myths of all of these ancient cultures is a mystery that has not been convincingly explained by historians of ancient religion. An intuitive answer is that the serpent originally came to prominence in one culture and then spread with a migrating populace to the other corners of the world. For that to be true—and for so many mythologies to take the same final form—the religion must have somehow evolved to a fairly advanced state in its original location and then spread in virtually all directions, supplanting any other preexisting traditions in those regions and leaving few traces of competing lines of development. Such a theory would lead us to wonder how the migrating tradition managed to overspread the various continents so completely yet leave the indigenous populations genetically distinct.

If the omnipresent serpent symbol is a good indicator of exactly how far the serpent tradition spread geographically, then so are many of the names by which various cultures called their deities. In some cases that have already been cited, the similarities between mythological names seem obvious. Yet even when the association between words seems less obvious, etymological examinations of the names bring us back to familiar roots from the Dogon and Egyptian creation stories, like po, amma, menu, min, and Dogon. This concurrence of the forms of names of gods and goddesses only lends further support to the idea that a single religious tradition somehow communicated itself across oceans and continents to the farthest reaches of the ancient world, as Godfrey Higgins noted in *Anacalypsis:*

> Buddha is variously pronounced and expressed *Boudh, Bod, Bot, But, Bad, Budd, Buddou, Boutta, Bota, Budso, Pot, Pout, Poti,* and *Pouti.* The Siamese make the final T or D quiescent, and sound the word *Po;* whence the Chinese still further vary it to Pho or Fo. In the Talmudic dialect the name is pronounced *Poden* or *Pooden.* . . . [Another] is *Min-Eswara,* formed by the same title *Min* or *Man* or *Menu* joined to *Eswara.* . . . [Another] is *Dagon* or *Dagun,* or *Dak-Po.* . . . *Wot* or *Vod* is a mere variation of *Bod;* and *Woden* [Odin] is simply the Talmudic mode of pronouncing Buddha.[18]

As we have noted, similarity of pronunciation in the Dogon tradition implies a relationship between mythological words. If we want to understand the relationships between myths of different cultures, it only makes sense to follow those similarities. Higgins continues:

> Amon is the *Om* of India, and *On* or . . . *an* of the Hebrews. . . . The word Am, Om, or Um, occurs in many languages, but has generally a meaning some way connected with the idea of a circle or cycle. . . . [T]here is a strong probability that the radical meaning of this word is cycle or circle. The name of the Supreme Being among the Brahmins of India is the first syllable only of this word pronounced AM. . . . The ancients had a precious stone called Ombria. It was supposed to have descended from heaven. . . . The word ON . . . is written in the Old Testament in two ways, *aun* and *an*. . . . This word is supposed to mean the sun . . . but I think it only stood for the sun as emblem of the procreative power of nature. . . . The word *am* in the Hebrew not only signifies might, strength, power, firmness, solidity, truth, but it means also *mother*, as in Genesis ii, 24. . . . If the word *am* [is taken to] mean mother, then a still more recondite idea will be implied, viz. the mother generative power, or the maternal generative power.[19]

Another prominent feature of the Dogon creation tradition that is found among many other ancient cultures is the concept of ancestral gods. Dogon myths tell about eight ancestors, one of whom was later killed, leaving seven surviving ancestors. During Griaule's instructional sessions, Ogotemmeli carefully explained that the story about the killing of the Dogon ancestor was only a parable used to illustrate a point (by our interpretation, an illustration of the mathematical concept of subtraction) and that no ancestor was actually killed. However, the story—if part of a global mythological tradition—serves to explain why some cultures retain a memory of eight ancestral gods but others only recall seven. We have already mentioned the Anunnaki of the Sumerians, the Egyptian Ogdoad, and the Elohim of Judaism as examples of these ancestral gods, but there are examples from other traditions that could also be included, like the Seven Sages of ancient China.

A final and perhaps a defining feature of ancient mythologies that seemingly crosses all global boundaries and borders is that of the pyramid. The pyramid as a symbolic structure is so widespread that it almost goes unnoticed as a mythological symbol that somehow might have been transmitted from region to region. Pyramids and pyramid -like structures are found in many different regions of the world, including the famous peaked pyramids of Giza and the well-known flat-topped pyramids of Mexico and Central America. Less well-known are the many pyramids found in Eastern Asia, such as the Xianyang pyramids of China, the Pulemelei stone pyramid of Samoa, or even the recently discovered Bosnian pyramid in Europe.[20] Some people include the ancient mounds of the British Isles and North America among the ranks of pyramidal structures. Much of the Dogon symbolism of the granary is reflected in pyramids of other regions. For instance, the Maya—like the Dogon—conceived of the pyramid as a woman lying on her back. These symbolic similarities extend even to the Dogon tradition of associating the four faces of the granary with star groups to watch over or control the agricultural cycle. Native American mounds were discussed by Sally A. Kitt Chappell in her online article, "Cahokia: Cosmic Landscape Architecture."

> The ancient Native Americans also took it upon themselves to construct places of similar importance. The mound-building culture of Cahokia, near East St. Louis, Missouri, built the largest mounded city in North America. Within the city limits, several particular structures can be speculated as to their astronomical significance in this culture. Cahokia's city plan appears to be laid out according to the cosmos: plazas and the largest mound are oriented in the cardinal directions, and the presence of several woodhenges that the ancient Americans used as solar calendars help to "determine when to hold ceremonies in preparation for planting, harvesting, and other events in the agricultural cycle and marked the all-important spring and fall equinox celebrations."[21]

It is important to note that the additional symbolism that attends the pyramid in some cultures—the star assignments meant to oversee the agricultural cycle and the notion of a pyramid as a woman lying on her back—argue against any theory of polygenesis (the idea that similar symbols evolved independently in various regions) as the source of globally used symbols of mythology. While it is entirely possible that two ancient cultures might independently choose to build pyramid-like structures, this kind of added symbolism does not follow logically from such a choice. Rather, it argues in favor of a preexisting symbolic system that was somehow transmitted to and adopted by these cultures.

THIRTEEN

FALL OF THE SERPENT RELIGION

I f we were to briefly recap the argument of this volume as presented up to this point, we might say that the well-preserved cosmological tradition of the Dogon defines an apparent system of mythological symbols and stories whose patterns we see repeated again and again in the myths and symbols of ancient cultures from widespread regions of the world. The Dogon explain their myths in the context of deliberate instruction that used key words, themes, and symbols that functioned cooperatively as sophisticated mnemonic devices and were closely intertwined with fundamental civilizing skills. These themes and symbols find expression in the routine acts of daily life such as weaving cloth, making a clay pot, and plowing a field.

Although our view is one of a global system of myth, it might not be enough to simply demonstrate the seemingly endless mythic and linguistic parallels found in so many contemporaneous ancient cultures. Nor might it be sufficient to show that so many of these cultures overtly credited knowledgeable ancestral teachers with having introduced these same early civilizing skills. Perhaps it is only coincidence (or else some deeply rooted human psychology) that causes them to say outright that their sophisticated symbolic systems were gifts presented to them by these same teacher-gods. To add further support to these many other evidences of a global mythic tradition—referred to by some as the serpent religion—we now admit statements from people of these same cultures, many of whom express parallel stories of how that ancient global tradition ended.

If we accept the many worldwide signs of the serpent religion as indicators of how far the religion spread geographically, then a natural question arises: What became of the serpent religion itself? The answer to this question might lie with another common mythological story line found in the serpent symbolism of many different cultures, both modern and ancient. This story tells how the serpents were transformed in the minds of the people within these cultures from deified ancestors to vilified fallen gods. This turnabout of events appears as a persistent theme among the oldest religions of the world, as we will demonstrate. For Griaule's instructor, Ogotemmeli, this episode was of the gravest historical importance, and he described it in detail to Griaule in one of their instructional sessions:

> Immediately after the smith, the first ancestor, the seven other ancestors descended. The ancestor of the leather-workers and the ancestor of the minstrels followed in order, each with his tools or instruments, and the other after them according to their rank. It was then that the incident occurred which was to determine the course of the reorganization.
>
> The eighth ancestor, breaking the order of precedence, came down before the seventh, the master of Speech. The latter was so greatly incensed that, on reaching the ground, he turned against the others and, in the form of a great serpent, made for the granary to take the seeds from it.
>
> According to another version, he bit the skin of the bellows in order to scatter the seeds which had been put in it. Others say that he came down at the same time as the smith in the form of the granary itself. On the ground he assumed the body of a great serpent, and a quarrel broke out between the two Spirits.
>
> Be that as it may, the smith, in order to rid himself of an adversary and carry out the great purposes of God, advised men to kill the snake and eat its body and give him the head.

"According to others," said Ogotemmeli, who attached the utmost importance to this turning-point in the history of the world and was concerned to make the attitude of the Spirits quite clear, "according to others the smith, on his arrival, found the men of the eight families, and set up his smithy in their midst. When he put down the skins of the bellows, the great serpent suddenly appeared and fell upon them, scattering the millet all around. The men, seeing this newcomer and taken aback by its action, killed it."[1]

Versions of a very similar event appear in the mythologies of many ancient societies. For the Egyptians, the story seems to describe a turning point at the end of the Old Kingdom (during the Second Intermediate Period, around 1600 BC) when widespread religious and cultural transition occurred. Some authorities such as James Bennett Pritchard suggest that there was great upheaval in Egypt at this time, perhaps connected with the massive eruption of the large volcano on the island of Thera. (Based on an examination of tree rings, dendochronologists [researchers who date ancient events by counting tree rings] Val LaMarche and Kathy Hirschboeck estimate that this occurred around 1628 BC.) Some people speculate that the effects of such an eruption could account for the stories of the ten plagues of Egypt at the time of the Exodus of the Hebrew slaves. An alternate viewpoint, based on controversial theories put forth by Immanuel Velikovsky in the 1950s, describes a global upheaval at this same time, the evidence of which is documented in his books *Worlds In Collision* and *Ages In Chaos*. This upheaval took the form of tremendous winds, storms, and tides. Velikovsky asserts that it was at this point in history when the words "typhoon," "cyclone," and "hurricane" entered the languages of the various nations of the world. Whatever the cause might have been, at about this time in history Egypt was driven under great duress to free its slaves and to make dramatic revisions in its own religion and society. Authorities such as Pritchard cite "The Prophecy of Neferti" (a papyrus text thought to have been written by a prophet early in the Middle Kingdom) as a description of the terrible destruction at this time.

The following translation of this narrative is quoted from Pritchard's
Ancient Near Eastern Texts:

> Behold, it is before thy face! Mayest thou rise up against what is
> before thee, for, behold, although great men are concerned with the
> land, what has been done is as what is not done. *Re must begin the
> foundation (of the earth over again).* The land is completely per-
> ished, (so that) no remainder exists, (so that) not (even) the black
> nail survives from what was fated.
>
> This land is (so) damaged (that) there is no one who is concerned
> with it, no one who speaks, no one who weeps. How is this land?
> The sun disc is covered over. It will not shine (so that) people
> may see. No one can live when clouds cover over (the sun). Then
> everybody is deaf for lack of it.
>
> I shall speak of what is before my face; I cannot foretell what has
> not (yet) come.
>
> The rivers of Egypt are empty, (so that) the water is crossed on
> foot. Men seek for water for the ships to sail on it. Its course is
> (become) a sandbank. The sandbank *is against* the flood; the place
> of water *is against* the flood; *(both)* the place of water *and* the
> sandbank. The south wind will oppose the north wind; the skies
> are no (longer) in a single wind. A foreign bird will be born in
> the marshes of the Northland. It has made a nest beside men, and
> people have let it approach through want of it. Damaged indeed
> are those good things, those fish-ponds, (where there were) those
> who clean fish, overflowing with fish and fowl. Everything good is
> disappeared, and the land is prostrate because of woes from that
> *food.* . . .
>
> This land is helter-skelter, and no one knows the result which
> will come about, which is hidden from speech, sight, or hearing.
> The face is deaf, for silence *confronts.* I show thee the land topsy-
> turvy. That which never happened has happened. . . .
>
> Re separates himself (from) mankind. If he shines forth, then
> the hour exists. No one knows when midday falls, for his shadow

cannot be distinguished. There is no one bright of face when seeing [him].[2]

In *Myth and Symbol in Ancient Egypt*, R. T. Rundle Clark quoted an Egyptian myth—again, similar to the Dogon story of the killing of the serpent—that tells about the turnabout of the attitude toward the formerly revered serpents from worship to vilification, which he ascribes to about this same historical time period—the approximate boundary between the Old and Middle Kingdoms of Egypt. It was a significant reversal that ultimately resulted in the ascendance of the god Thoth as the primary state god of Egypt:

A myth which probably dates from the early Middle Kingdom, describes how the power of the primeval snakes was curtailed.

This God (i.e., Atum) called to Thoth, saying: "Summon Geb to me, saying, 'Come, hurry!'" So when Geb had come to him, he said:

"Take care of the serpents which are in you. Behold, they showed respect for me while I was down there. But now you have learned their [real] nature. Proceed to the place where Father Nun is, tell him to keep guard over the serpents, whether in the earth or in the water. Also you must write it down that it is your task to go wherever your serpents are and say: 'See that you do no damage!' They must know that I am still here (in the world) and that I have put a seal upon them. Now their lot is to be in the world for ever. But beware of the magical spells which their mouths know, for Hike is himself therein. But knowledge is in you. It will not come about that I, in my greatness, will have to keep guard over them as I once did, but I will hand them over to your son Osiris so that he can watch over their children and the hearts of their fathers be made to forget. Thus advantage can come from them, out of what they perform for love of the whole world, through the magical power that is in them."[3]

Based on such texts, it would seem that as a consequence of major upheaval in the Egyptian culture, the historical reverence of the Egyptians for the serpent gods ended and a newfound fear of them emerged. Some researchers like Velikovsky assign the Exodus of the Jews from Egypt to this same time period, and there is a linguistic connection that might help to affirm this. In the Egyptian hieroglyphic language, the word *shamash* means "Sirius," the star most intimately associated with the serpent gods, and the word *shaa-mes* means "firstborn."[4] In Judaism, the tenth plague associated with the Exodus from Egypt was the slaying of the firstborn. What this implies is that the story of the tenth plague (recalling that ten is considered the number of the serpent god) might well refer to the fall of the serpent teachers associated with Sirius. In his book, Clark described the vilification of the serpents.

> The serpents are the demonic, chaotic powers who dwell in the lower world. As long as the High God dwelt in the Abyss or on earth they were under control, but after the rebellion of mankind he departed to the sky. The serpents thought that God no longer existed and began to show their true colors. He therefore sent Geb down to them with a written message. They were to keep within the earth, where they would live eternally. They have power—Hike—but Geb, with his written instructions, has knowledge. This is the oldest statement of the belief that the forces of nature have to be curbed by "knowledge." . . . Ultimately, the task of curbing the serpents devolves on Osiris. This is a strange statement, because Osiris is usually passive and his theology cannot be reconciled with the concept of nature found in this myth. . . . There is an echo of a similar belief in the "Great Quarrel" where Osiris has to keep in check the denizens of the Underworld.[5]

Linguistic comparisons provide us with an interesting explanation for another famous episode from the story of the Exodus, in which Moses is presented to the Egyptian pharaoh and is said to turn his staff into a serpent. An alternate interpretation from the Egyptian perspective is that Moses demonstrated that he knew the secrets of the serpent. In Egyptian hieroglyphic passages in which the pharaoh speaks to the gods or the gods speak to the pharaoh, it is traditional for the passage to begin with a hieroglyph that consists of a serpent and a staff.

The fall of the serpent religion has another possible implication related to the time of the Exodus. If that event was related to the overthrow of the serpent gods of Egypt, it is completely understandable that the first commandment given by God to Moses would have been, "Thou shalt have no other gods before me," because it would have been a specific injunction against the former serpent gods. It would also explain why this same God would require as tribute the ritual sacrifice of a ram—an animal that was a symbol of the former god.

As support for the testimony of myth to the dramatic events of the fall of the serpent religion, Michael Rice tells us in *Egypt's Making: The Origins of Ancient Egypt* about likely physical evidence of this same dramatic fall from favor of previous kings after the First Dynasty of Egypt:

> At some time after the end of the dynasty all the tombs in which the Kings and high officials were buried, on the escarpment at Saqqara looking down on Memphis, at Abydos, and at Helwan, were destroyed in immense conflagrations. The fires were intense and the destruction of the houses of these great dead was without doubt deliberate. Their memory seems to have been so abominated that all trace of them had to be obliterated. Somehow the customary explanation, of dynastic upheavals and the vindictiveness of their political opponents, seems inadequate for so violent a manifestation of hate and rejection carried out with such ruthless determination over the whole country.[6]

Based on these texts, it is quite easy to see how the serpent, which was eventually relegated in the Egyptian religion to the realm of the underworld, came to represent the fallen angel of Christianity. The symbols of the Nummo, now seen in a new context, are also the symbols of the devil in Christendom—a horned former deity with a tail like a serpent. We can even find within Dogon mythology a link to the Christian name of this fallen god—Satan—as well as a possible link to a name for God that was used in Judaism. It was mentioned in a previous chapter that the Dogon call their creation myth "aduno so tanie" (history of the universe). From a linguistic standpoint, the word *aduno* is remarkably close to the Hebrew word *adonai,* which is used as a name for God; the phrase *so tanie* is similarly close to the name Satan. Direct support for this interpretation can be found in *The Book of the Secrets of Enoch,* an alternate scriptural text included in *The Other Bible,* edited by Willis Barnstone:

> The Devil is the evil spirit of the lower places, a fugitive. He made Sotana from the heavens, so his name was Satomail. Thus he became different from the angels, but his nature did not change his intelligence in regard to understanding right and wrong. Therefore he nurtured thoughts against Adam. He entered his world and seduced Eva but did not touch Adam. I cursed ignorance. But what I had blessed previously, that I did not curse—not man, nor the earth, nor other creatures, but man's evil fruit and works.
>
> I said to him "You are earth, and into the earth from which I took you, you shall go, and I shall not destroy you but send you away from where I placed you."[7]

In the Americas, the Aztecs tell similar stories of the fall of the serpent god Quetzalcoatl, only in this case—as in the Dogon myth—the serpent continues to play the role of an exiled benefactor and does not become conceptualized as a villainous god who is cast into the underworld. Neil Baldwin provided a summary of this Aztec tale in *Legends of the Plumed Serpent:*

> Every hero must have his downfall . . . every illuminating state of grace requires a dark and cloudy consequence, every benign force engenders an evil one. In the Plumed Serpent's story, the evil force assumed the shape of his own brother, Tezcatlipoca, "Smoking

Mirror." He was the *hechicero,* the "somber sorcerer," the adversary "capable of inconceivable deeds" and possessed of "the secret knowledge of the seer," allowing him to cast a spell on his victims. What more threatening name could there be for this doppelganger, this foe of goodness, than the "evil twin," the demonic alter ego of Plumed Serpent?

Some codices say that the resentful Smoking Mirror defeated the good Quetzalcoatl in a "magical duel." Others say the Plumed Serpent was duped into sleeping with his own sister after drinking *pulque* prepared by Smoking Mirror and his cohorts. After a fierce struggle, the beloved ruler of the spirit realm—man of classic Toltec knowledge—was lured into drunkenness and carnality, brought down by the polluting, corrupt, and worldly wiles of the trickster. . . .

Like the planet Venus, the sign of his transfiguration in the cosmic cycle—like the very earth itself, passing in and out of rainy and dry seasons—Plumed Serpent was fated to die and be reborn over and over again, through eternity.

For now, however, the only path for the victim of temptation was expulsion and exile. Such a dire fate caused deep anxiety among the people Plumed Serpent had so devotedly taught.

"Why do you leave your capital?"

"I go to *Tlapallan,*" replied Quetzalcoatl, "from whence I came."

"For what reason?" persisted the enchanters.

"My partner the sun has called me thence," replied Quetzalcoatl.

"Go then, happily," they said, "but leave us the secret of your art, the secret of founding in silver, of working in precious stones and woods, of painting, and of feather-working, and other matters."

Tlapallan is a variant of *Tlili Tlapali,* Nahua for "land of the red and black," the name given to writing, glyphs, and mural paintings. Learning through these means at the feet of Quetzalcoatl, who possessed sovereignty over intellectual matters, mankind first gained wisdom.[8]

No matter which legend of which of these ancient cultures we choose to believe, a consistent pattern of events is made plainly clear. A knowledgeable, godlike teacher who was associated with the symbol of the serpent taught mankind the rudiments of civilization—agriculture, weaving, language, mathematics, science, and the skills of the arts and crafts. After a period of time living among them and having imparted these civilizing skills, the teacher either left or was driven out—an event that is seen by culture after culture as a turning point in the history of the world.

FOURTEEN

CONCLUSION

The information presented in the preceding chapters demonstrates a direct relationship between the symbols and themes of the Dogon creation story and known scientific facts relating to the formation of the universe, matter, and biological reproduction. This relationship is a broad and specific one that is couched in clear definitions and supported by priestly interpretations and cosmological drawings. The parallels between Dogon myth and science run deep. The Dogon concepts touch on virtually every salient point of the related science and do so in organized and sensible ways. Moreover, the extended parallels between myth and science sustain themselves through complex discussions of the formative processes of the universe and the conception of life.

Correlations between the Dogon myths and science begin with explicit statements by the Dogon priests, which establish that the esoteric tradition of the Dogon is specifically understood to describe the underlying processes by which matter and life were formed. Details of these processes then play out in parallel with modern scientific theory, matching the components and component processes of myth with those of science. This kind of direct correlation with known facts taken in any context other than that of ancient myth would surely be accepted as a positive statement of real knowledge.

It should be emphasized that the scientific interpretations we place on various Dogon cosmological symbols are not arbitrary ones. Rather, they are driven by and are consistent with the ways in which the Dogon elders understand and define their own symbols. These interpretations are aided by the definition of cosmological keywords such as *po, sene, bummo, yala, tonu,* and *toymu*—and by symbolic keywords such as "Water," "Fire," "Wind," and "Earth." Such words seem to transcend boundaries of culture, and their likely counterparts in the Egyptian hieroglyphic language often confirm the scientific sense of meaning assigned to the words by the Dogon. In the purest cases, these relationships between words are supported by common multiple meanings or by common related symbols—often by the Egyptian glyphs used to write the words, whose shapes match related Dogon cosmological drawings.

The coherence of Dogon cosmology is upheld by a sensible, well-defined system of symbolic storylines whose themes directly mirror the best modern scientific theories of how the universe and matter might have actually come to exist. The myths express themselves clearly and succinctly, so much so that the statements of the Dogon priests are often most easily understood in direct comparison with comparable statements from popular modern interpreters of science—authors of the caliber of Stephen Hawking, Brian Greene, and Richard Feynman. Our understanding of these statements by Dogon priests is guided and supported by important cosmological drawings that often appear in a similar context and take the same form as related scientific diagrams.

The Dogon symbols and concepts relating to atomic structure so thoroughly mimic their scientific counterparts that, if our purpose was to refute their basis in science, we would first need to explain in some believable way the following extraordinary similarities:

- The po, which is defined in terms similar to those that describe the atom
- Sene seeds, which are described in form and behavior as being similar to protons, neutrons, and electrons and whose "nesting" is recognizable as an electron orbit
- The germination of the sene, whose drawn images are a match for the four types of quantum spin particles
- The spider of the sene whose threads weave the 266 seeds of

Amma, much as string theory tells us all matter is woven from strings

- The basic creative impulse of the gods, from whom all of these particles emerged, which is stated in terms that run parallel to the concept of the four basic quantum forces

In many previous examples, this study has demonstrated a consistent relationship between symbols and concepts of the Dogon people and modern science. These examples show, among other things, that the Dogon myths clearly describe:

- The correct attributes of the unformed universe
- That all matter was created by the opening of the universe
- That spiraling galaxies of stars were formed when the universe opened
- That this same event was responsible for the creation of light and time
- The complex relationship between light and time
- That matter can behave like a particle or as a wave
- That sound travels in waves
- That matter is composed of fundamental components
- The correct counts of the elements within each component category of matter
- That the most basic component of matter is a thread
- That this fundamental thread vibrates
- That under some conditions threads can form membranes
- That threads give rise to the four fundamental quantum forces
- The correct attributes of these quantum forces
- The correct attributes of the four types of quantum spin particles
- The concept of the uncertainty principle
- That atoms are formed from smaller particles
- That electrons orbit atoms
- That component particles other than electrons make up the nucleus of an atom

- The correct shape of an electron orbit
- That electrons of one atom can be "stolen" by other atoms to form molecular bond
- That light is emitted by changes in the energy level of an electron
- The correct electron structures of water and of copper
- That hydrogen atoms form pairs
- That sunlight is the result of the fusion of hydrogen atoms
- That water goes through phase transitions
- That the emergence of matter in the universe is related to phase transitions
- The correct steps in the natural water cycle
- That the first single cell emerged spontaneously from water
- That cells reproduce by mitosis to form two twin cells
- The correct sequence of events during sexual reproduction and growth of an embryo
- That female and male contributions are required for sexual reproduction
- That children inherit genetic characteristics from each parent
- That there are 22 chromosome pairs
- That sex is determined by the X and Y chromosomes
- That chromosomes move apart and spindles form during mitosis
- The correct shapes and attributes of chromosomes and spindles
- That sexual reproduction starts with the formation of germ cells
- That germ cells reproduce by a process unique to themselves
- That eggs live longer than other cells
- The correct configuration and attributes of DNA

Given the tribal nature of Dogon society, we might be inclined—as was Carl Sagan—to ascribe any apparent Dogon scientific knowledge to recent contacts with modern cultures. However, upon closer examination, we see that this point of view simply does not hold water. The Dogon cosmological system conveys scientific meaning through a complex system of mythological themes, symbols, storylines, and words. Time and again, we have shown that these same symbolic elements existed in similar form among the 5,000-year-old mythologies of early cultures from widely separated regions of the earth. The suggestion that this science was conveyed to the Dogon through modern contacts does not adequately explain the presence of these same well-known symbols in ancient myths. The Dogon also profess knowledge of a number of scientific facts that were not known, and others that were not even proposed, by modern science when they were documented by Griaule and Dieterlen in the 1930s, 1940s, and 1950s. These statements of apparent fact also serve to undermine any suggestion that the Dogon could have derived their knowledge from contact with modern sources.

It is important to note that Dogon society carries with it ample signs of an ancient lineage. This can be readily seen in the cultural and linguistic similarities between the Dogon and the people of ancient Egypt, which would be expected of two closely related cultures. The concurrence of these same cultural features among the Amazigh, whose culture is known to date from the earliest days of ancient Egypt, argues in favor of a long history for the Dogon. The Dogon people also observe more than a fair share of rituals and traditions typically associated with ancient Egypt and other elder societies, such as the cultural imperative to build aligned structures, the use of a 360-day calendar, and so on. Other likely relationships to ancient Egypt can be seen in Dogon agricultural practices, in their societal reverence for ancestors, in their peculiarly Egyptian-like civic organization, and in details of their astronomical knowledge.

Other aspects of Dogon cosmology argue for an early relationship between the Dogon and ancient Egyptian mythological systems. For instance, the Dogon tradition of eight ancestors seems to bear a relationship to the Egyptian Ogdoad, and yet the Dogon do not assign actual god or goddess names to these ancestors. Likewise, there seems to be a relationship between Dogon cosmological drawings and the shapes of various Egyptian glyphs, yet among the Dogon, these drawings have never taken on the status of an actual written language. Dada, the Dogon spider who weaves matter and whose name means "mother" in the Dogon language, exhibits many of the classical attributes of the

Egyptian (and Amazigh) goddess Neith. In fact, other ancient goddesses, like Athena, who are traditionally associated with Neith also are associated with spider symbolism similar to that found in Dogon cosmology. Such consistencies suggest that the Dogon system of myth could represent an early incarnation of the Egyptian myths.

The clear implication of the Dogon myths and their apparent relationship to science is that, at some point prior to 3400 BC, mankind was the beneficiary of deliberate civilizing instruction presented (if the Dogon account is to be believed) by careful, well-meaning, knowledgeable teachers. Such instruction could account for the apparently sudden rise of Egyptian civilization from the backdrop of earlier hunter tribes. It could also account for the numerous cultural histories of ancestor-teacher-gods found around the world. The myths, symbols, traditions, symbolic languages, and shrines of ancient cultures—the mnemonic devices by which this instruction was seemingly transmitted and sustained—are the apparent evidence of this instruction, and the serpent—an Egyptian symbol for "the Word"—is the teacher's signature icon.

If the impulse to associate the various ancient world mythologies with a single planned mythological system is driven by apparent similarities between myths of ancient societies, then the confirmation of such a relationship lies in what—to all logical modes of thought—should be their apparent differences, had they actually arisen independently of each other. For example, it is clear that the mere impulse on the part of an ancient society to build a structure that was aligned with the stars would not logically dictate (Jung notwithstanding) a mythology that expresses itself in terms of archetypical symbols such as water, fire, wind, and earth. Nor is there compelling reason for that same culture to adopt a belief that the civilizing skills of humanity were imparted to them by ancestral teachers. Likewise, there would be no automatic reason for such a culture to assert that written language was a gift from these same teachers. To my way of thinking, one critical omission on the part of most researchers of ancient myth has been to ignore these unexplained similarities, which seem to coexist among widely divergent societies but without compelling reason. These unreasoned connections function like fingerprints found at a crime scene. Often, they are what enable us to positively align parallel ancient mythologies. In my view, these kinds of connections, perhaps along with undiscovered relationships of ancient language, are the likely foundation upon which to build future arguments in favor of a global ancient system of instructional myth.

NOTES

Introduction

1. Griaule and Dieterlen, *The Pale Fox*, 23–39.

Chapter 2: Themes of the Ancient Creation Stories

1. Caubet and Pouyssegur, *The Ancient Near East*, 172.
2. Budge, *The Gods of the Egyptians*, 290.
3. Grimal, *A History of Ancient Egypt*, 45.

Chapter 3: The Dogon Creation Story

1. Griaule, *Conversations with Ogotemmeli*, 19.

Chapter 4: Dogon Symbols and Meanings

1. Griaule and Dieterlen, *The Pale Fox*, 57–60.
2. Ibid., 61.
3. Ibid., 70.
4. Griaule and Dieterlen, "The Dogon," 83.
5. Griaule, *Conversations with Ogotemmeli*, 19.
6. Ibid., 107.
7. Pritchard, *Ancient Near Eastern Texts*, 3.
8. Cowen, "Found: Primordial Water," 284.
9. Wu, "Buckyballs Can Come from Outer Space," 196.
10. Griaule and Dieterlen, *The Pale Fox*, 54.

Chapter 5: Dogon Parallels to the Big Bang and Atomic and Quantum Structure

1. Dozier, *Codes of Evolution*, 7–8.
2. Griaule and Dieterlen, *The Pale Fox*, 101, 105.
3. Hawking, *A Brief History of Time*, 81–86.
4. Weiss, "Seeking the Mother of All Matter," 138.
5. Griaule and Dieterlen, *The Pale Fox*, 130–31.
6. Weiss, "Seeking the Mother of All Matter," 138.

7. Calame-Griaule, *Dictionnaire Dogon*, 228. "Le fonio joue un role tres important dans la cosmologie dogon. Image de l'atome dont est sorti l'univers, il porte sur sa graine de petites stries qui figurent l'eclatement de la graine et le monde se propageant en spirale."
8. Feynman, *The Character of Physical Law*, 128.
9. Griaule and Dieterlen, *The Pale Fox*, 95.
10. Ibid., 95–96.
11. Ibid., 95–96.
12. Hawking, *A Brief History of Time*, 69–72.
13. Griaule and Dieterlen, *The Pale Fox*, 132–34.
14. Hawking, *A Brief History of Time*, 66–67.
15. Ibid., 67.
16. Griaule and Dieterlen, *The Pale Fox*, 110.
17. Griaule, *Conversations with Ogotemmeli*, 42.
18. Hawking, *A Brief History of Time*, 121.
19. Griaule and Dieterlen, *The Pale Fox*, 93.
20. Hawking, *A Brief History of Time*, 65.

Chapter 6: Dogon Parallels to String Theory

1. Greene, *The Elegant Universe*, 14.
2. Ibid., 143.
3. Marcel Griaule and Germaine Dieterlen, "The Dogon," 84.
4. Griaule and Dieterlen, *The Pale Fox*, 108.
5. Ibid., 236.
6. Ibid., 236–37.
7. Greene, *The Elegant Universe*, 315.
8. Griaule and Dieterlen, *The Pale Fox*, 417.
9. Basan and Basan, "String Theory and M-Theory," http://www.galactica2003 .net/colonials/spacefolding.shtml.
10. Griaule and Dieterlen, *The Pale Fox*, 137–38.
11. Greene, *The Elegant Universe*, 332.

Chapter 7: Dogon Parallels to Egyptian Mythology

1. Hart, *A Dictionary of Egyptian Gods and Goddesses*, 179.
2. Higgins, *Anacalypsis*, 318.
3. Sauneron, *The Priests of Ancient Egypt*, 125–27.
4. Temple, *The Sirius Mystery*, 175.
5. Budge, *An Egyptian Hieroglyphic Dictionary*, 266b.
6. Hart, *A Dictionary of Egyptian Gods and Goddesses*, 213.
7. Krauss, *Atom: An Odyssey From the Big Bang to Life on Earth . . . and Beyond*, 72.
8. Quirke, *Ancient Egyptian Religion*, 25.
9. Grimal, *A History of Ancient Egypt*, 41–42.
10. Wake, "The Origin of Serpent Worship," 45.
11. Saggs, *Civilization Before Greece and Rome*, 51.

12. Grimal, *A History of Ancient Egypt*, 126.
13. Budge, *An Egyptian Hieroglyphic Dictionary*, 217a.
14. Ibid., 723a.
15. Ibid., 683a.
16. Hawking, A *Brief History of Time*, 65.
17. Budge, *Legends of the Egyptian Gods*, xvii.
18. Seleem, *The Illustrated Egyptian Book of the Dead*, 35.
19. Budge, *An Egyptian Hieroglyphic Dictionary*, 859ab.
20. Griffis-Greenberg, *Neith: Goddess of the Beginning, the Beyond, and the End*, http://www.geocities.com/Athens/Acropolis/8669/neith.html.

Chapter 8: Dogon Parallels to Genetics and Sexual Reproduction

1. Griaule and Dieterlen, *The Pale Fox*, 84.
2. Bauval and Gilbert, *The Orion Mystery*, 17.
3. Griaule and Dieterlen, *The Pale Fox*, 121–22.
4. Ibid., 161–62.
5. Temple, *The Sirius Mystery*, 85.
6. Ibid., 94.
7. Black and Green, *Gods, Demons and Symbols of Ancient Mesopotamia*, 34.
8. Griaule and Dieterlen, *The Pale Fox*, 165.
9. Ibid., 123.
10. Dozier, *Codes of Evolution*, 7.
11. Griaule and Dieterlen, *The Pale Fox*, 126.
12. Dozier, *Codes of Evolution*, 36.
13. Ibid., 29.

Chapter 9: Archaeology and Dogon Symbols

1. "Seshat, Female Scribe, Goddess of Writing Measurement," Caroline Seawright, http://www.touregypt.net/featurestories/seshat.htm.
2. "Ancient Gods—The Olympians," Hellas OnLine, http://www.hol.gr/greece/olymp.htm.
3. Mercantante, *Facts on File Encyclopedia of World Mythology and Legend*, 226.
4. Grimal, *A History of Ancient Egypt*, 51.
5. Temple, *The Sirius Mystery*, 3.
6. *The Egyptian Book of the Dead*, http://www.american-buddha.com/egyptbookofdead8.htm?signup#SPEECH%20OF%20NEPHTHYS.
7. Tompkins, *Secrets of the Great Pyramid*. British engineer J. H. Cole also conducted a survey of the dimensions of the Great Pyramid in 1925.
8. Gill, *The Great Pyramid Speaks*, 22.
9. Tompkins, *Secrets of the Great Pyramid*, 70–72.
10. Grimal, *A History of Ancient Egypt*, 51.
11. Griaule and Dieterlen, *The Pale Fox*, 360.
12. Ibid., 364–65.

13. Jacq, *Fascinating Hieroglyphs*, 129.
14. Clark, *Myth and Symbol in Ancient Egypt*, 225.

Chapter 10: Judaism and Dogon Symbols

1. Budge, *An Egyptian Hieroglyphic Dictionary*, 615b.
2. Griaule and Dieterlen, "A Sudanese Sirius System," from Temple, *The Sirius Mystery*, 40.
3. Trepp, *The Complete Book of Jewish Observance*, 219–20. Reprinted with permission, www. behrmanhouse.com.
4. Griaule and Dieterlen, "A Sudanese Sirius System," from Temple, *The Sirius Mystery*, 40.
5. Ibid., 40–41.
6. Herodotus, *Histories*, http://www.bostonleadershipbuilders.com/herodotus/book02.htm.
7. Budge, *An Egyptian Hieroglyphic Dictionary*, 870, 871.
8. Ibid., 819a.
9. Higgins, *Anacalypsis*, 311.
10. Herodotus, *Histories*, http://www.bostonleadershipbuilders.com/herodotus/book02.htm.
11. Ibid.
12. Higgins, *Anacalypsis*, 72–73.
13. Barnstone, *The Other Bible*, 11.
14. Ouaknin, *Symbols of Judaism*, 14.
15. Clarke, *Siva and Serpent Worship*, ix–x.
16. Moore, *Judaism in the First Centuries of the Christian Era*, 364–66.
17. Higgins, *Anacalypsis*, 62.
18. Ibid., 64–71.
19. Trepp, *The Complete Book of Jewish Observance*, 28–30.
20. Ouaknin, *Symbols of Judaism*, 20.
21. Moore, *Judaism in the First Centuries of the Christian Era*, 415–18.
22. Ibid., 383.

Chapter 11: The Dogon Concept of Light

1. Hawking, *A Brief History of Time*, 20–21.
2. Budge, *An Egyptian Hieroglyphic Dictionary*, 23a.
3. Griaule and Dieterlen, *The Pale Fox*, 198–99.
4. Budge, *An Egyptian Hieroglyphic Dictionary*, 608b.
5. Hawking, *A Brief History of Time*, 21.
6. Griaule and Dieterlen, *The Pale Fox*, 204.
7. Budge, *An Egyptian Hieroglyphic Dictionary*, 255b.
8. Griaule and Dieterlen, *The Pale Fox*, 201.
9. Ibid., 200–201.
10. Ibid., 202.
11. Hagan, *The Shining Ones*, 15.
12. Budge, *An Egyptian Hieroglyphic Dictionary*, 23ab.

Chapter 12: Global Signs of the Serpent Religion

1. "Our 5000 Year Heritage: The Inuit Regions," http://www.itk.ca/5000-year heritage/index.php; "Archaeological Survey of Canada," http://www.civilization .ca/cmc/archeo/oracles/grbear/056e.htm; "History of the American Indians," http://www.historyworld.net/wrldhis/PlainTextHistories.asp?HistoryID=ab05; Dr. Robert Churchill, "Ancient China," http://mockingbird.creighton.edu/ worldlit/works/churchill/china.htm.

2. Cotterell and Storm, *The Ultimate Encyclopedia of Mythology*, 356.

3. Ibid., 444.

4. Miller and Taube, *The Gods and Symbols of Ancient Mexico and the Maya*, 134.

5. Ibid., 41.

6. Ibid., 132.

7. Long, *The Myths of Creation*, 65.

8. Best, *Maori Religion and Mythology*, 32–34.

9. Miller and Taube, *The Gods and Symbols of Ancient Mexico and the Maya*, 156.

10. Ibid., 162.

11. Clarke, *Serpent and Siva Worship and Mythology in Central America, Africa and Asia*, vi.

12. Wake, "The Origin of Serpent Worship," 39–43.

13. Hamilton, *Mythology: Timeless Tales of Gods and Heroes*, 65–68.

14. Bulfinch, *Age of Fable*, 3.

15. Wake, "The Origin of Serpent Worship," 41.

16. Cotterell and Storm, *The Ultimate Encyclopedia of Mythology*, 468.

17. Miller and Taube, *The Gods and Symbols of Ancient Mexico and the Maya*, 148–50.

18. Higgins, *Anacalypsis*, 153.

19. Ibid., 109–10.

20. "Europe's First Pyramid Discovered in Bosnia," http://www.rumormillnews. com/cgi-bin/forum.cgi?read=80951.

21. Chappell, Sally A. Kitt, "Cahokia: Cosmic Landscape Architecture," http:// www.press.uchicago.edu/Misc/Chicago/101363.html.

Chapter 13: Fall of the Serpent Religion

1. Griaule, *Conversations with Ogotemmeli*, 45–46.

2. Pritchard, *Ancient Near Eastern Texts*, 445–46.

3. Clark, *Myth and Symbol in Ancient Egypt*, 243–44.

4. Budge, *An Egyptian Hieroglyphic Dictionary*, 723a.

5. Clark, *Myth and Symbol in Ancient Egypt*, 244.

6. Rice, *Egypt's Making: The Origins of Ancient Egypt*, 129.

7. Barnstone, *The Other Bible*, 6.

8. Baldwin, *Legends of the Plumed Serpent*, 34–35.

BIBLIOGRAPHY

Allen, James P. *An Introduction to the Language and Culture of the Hieroglyphs.* Cambridge: Cambridge University Press, 2000.

Aveni, Anthony. *Stairways to the Stars.* New York: John Wiley & Sons, Inc., 1997.

Baldwin, Neil. *Legends of the Plumed Serpent.* New York: Public Affairs, 1998.

Barnstone, Willis. *The Other Bible.* San Francisco: Harper San Francisco, 1984.

Basan, Markus, and Claus Basan. *"String Theory and M-Theory."* http://www. galactia2003.net/colonials/spacefolding.shtml.

Bauval, Robert, and Adrian Gilbert. *The Orion Mystery.* New York: Crown Publishers, Inc., 1994.

Begley, Sharon, and Thomas Hayden. "How It All Started," *Newsweek,* May 8, 2000, 48–49.

Best, Elsdon. *Maori Religion and Mythology.* Wellington, New Zealand: W. A. G. Skinner, Government Printer, 1924.

Black, Jeremy, and Anthony Green. *Gods, Demons and Symbols of Ancient Mesopotamia.* Austin: University of Texas Press, 1997.

Budge, E. A. Wallis. *An Egyptian Hieroglyphic Dictionary.* New York: Dover, 1978.

———. *Egyptian Language—Lessons in Egyptian Hieroglyphics.* New York: Dorset Press, 1993.

———. *The Gods of the Egyptians.* New York: Dover, 1994.

———. *Legends of the Egyptian Gods.* New York: Dover, 1994.

Bulfinch, Thomas. *Age of Fable.* New York: Dell Publishing Co., 1959.

Calame-Griaule, Genevieve. *Dictionnaire Dogon.* Paris: Librarie C. Klincksieck, 1968.

Caubet, Annie, and Patrick Pouyssegur. *The Ancient Near East.* Paris: Terrail, 1997; English edition, Paderborn, Italy: Bayard Presse SA, 1998.

Clark, R. T. Rundle. *Myth and Symbol in Ancient Egypt.* London: Thames and Hudson, 1995.

Clarke, Hyde. *Serpent and Siva Worship and Mythology in Central America, Africa and Asia.* New York: J. W. Bouten, 1877.

Cotterell, Arthur, and Rachel Storm. *The Ultimate Encyclopedia of Mythology.* London: Lorenz Books, 1999.

Cowen, Ron. "Found: Primordial Water." *Science News,* 156, no. 18 (1999).

Davies, Paul, and John Gribben. *The Matter Myth.* New York: Simon & Schuster/ Touchstone, 1992.

Dozier, Rush W., Jr. *Codes of Evolution.* New York: Crown Publishers, Inc., 1992.

Duncan, David Ewing. *Calendar.* New York: Avon Books, Inc., 1998.

Encarta 97 Encyclopedia, Microsoft, 1993–1996.

Feynman, Richard P. *The Character of Physical Law.* Boston: MIT Press, 1967.

Forde, Daryll. *African Worlds.* London: Oxford University Press, 1954. Reprinted with a new introduction by Wendy James, James Currey Publishers and LIT Verlag for the International African Institute, 1999.

Gill, Joseph B. *The Great Pyramid Speaks.* New York: Barnes & Noble Books, 1984.

Graves, Robert. *New Larousse Encyclopedia of Mythology.* London: Hamlyn Publishing Group Limited, 1968.

Greene, Brian. *The Elegant Universe.* New York: Vintage Books, 2000.

Griaule, Marcel. *Conversations with Ogotemmeli.* Oxford: Oxford University Press, 1970.

Griaule, Marcel, and Germaine Dieterlen. "The Dogon." In *African Worlds: Studies in the Cosmological Ideas and Social Values of African Peoples.* London: Oxford University Press, 1954, 83–110.

———. *The Pale Fox.* Chino Valley, AZ: Continuum Foundation, 1986. First published as *Le renard pale.* Paris: l'Intitut d'Ethnologie, 1965.

———. "A Sudanese Sirius System." In *The Sirius Mystery,* Robert K. G. Temple, Rochester, VT: Destiny Books, 1987, 35–51.

Griffis-Greenberg, Katherine. *Neith: Goddess of the Beginning, the Beyond, and the End.* http://www.geocities.com/Athens/Acropolis/ 8669/neith.html.

Grimal, Nicholas. *A History of Ancient Egypt.* Oxford, UK, and Cambridge, MA: Blackwell, 1994.

Hagan, Helene. *The Shining Ones.* Philadelphia: Xlibris, 2000.

Hamilton, Edith. *Mythology: Timeless Tales of Gods and Heroes.* New York: Warner Books, 1999.

Hancock, Graham. *Fingerprints of the Gods.* New York Crown Publishers, Inc., 1995.

Hancock, Graham, and Robert Bauval. *The Message of the Sphinx.* New York: Crown Publishers, Inc., 1996.

Hapgood, Charles. *Maps of the Ancient Sea Kings.* Kempton, IL: Adventures Unlimited Press, 1966.

Hart, George. *A Dictionary of Egyptian Gods and Goddesses.* London and New York: Routledge, 1999.

Hawking, Stephen W. *A Brief History of Time.* Toronto: Bantam Books, 1988.

Higgins, Godfrey. *Anacalypsis.* 1833. Reprint, Whitefish, MT: Kessinger Publishing Company, 2002.

Jacq, Christian. *Fascinating Hieroglyphs.* New York: Sterling Publishing Co, Inc., 1996.

Krauss, Lawrence M. *Atom: An Odyssey from the Big Bang to Life on Earth . . . and Beyond.* Boston, New York, and London: Little, Brown and Company, 2001.

Long, Charles H. *Alpha: The Myths of Creation.* New York: George Braziller, 1963.

Mercantante, Anthony S. *Facts on File Encyclopedia of World Mythology and Legend.* New York and Oxford: Facts On File, 1988.

Merriam-Webster's Encyclopedia of World Religions. Springfield, MA: Merriam-Webster, 1999.

Miller, Mary, and Karl Taube. *The Gods and Symbols of Ancient Mexico and the Maya.* London: Thames and Hudson, 1993.

Moore, George Foot. *Judaism in the First Centuries of the Christian Era.* Vol. 1, *The Age of Tannaim.* New York: Schocken Books, 1971.

Ouaknin, Marc-Alain. *Symbols of Judaism.* New York: Assouline Publishing, 2000.

Pritchard, James B. *Ancient Near Eastern Texts,* 3rd ed. Princeton, NJ: Princeton University Press, 1969.

Quirke, Stephen. *Ancient Egyptian Religion.* London: British Museum Press, 1992.

Rice, Michael. *Egypt's Making: The Origins of Ancient Egypt, 5000–2000 BC.* London: Routledge, 1991.

Saggs, H. W. F. *Civilization Before Greece and Rome.* New Haven and London: Yale University Press, 1989.

Sauneron, Serge. *The Priests of Ancient Egypt.* Ithaca and London: Cornell University Press, 2000.

Seleem, R. Ramses. *The Illustrated Egyptian Book of the Dead.* New York: Sterling Publishing Company, Inc., 2001.

Temple, Robert K. G. *The Sirius Mystery.* Rochester, VT: Destiny Books, 1987.

Tompkins, Peter. *Secrets of the Great Pyramid.* New York: Galahad Books, 1971.

Trepp, Leo. *The Complete Book of Jewish Observance.* New York: Summit Books, 1980, 1981.

Velikovsky, Immanuel. *Ages in Chaos.* Garden City, NY: Doubleday & Company, Inc., 1952.

———. *Oedipus and Akhnaton.* Garden City, NY: Doubleday & Company, Inc., 1960.

———. *Worlds in Collision.* New York: The MacMillan Company, 1950.

Vergani, Teresa. *Ethnomathematics and Symbolic Thought: The Culture of the Dogon.* http://emis.u-strasbg.fr//journals/ZDM/zdm992a4.pdf.

Wake, C. Staniland. "The Origin of Serpent Worship." In *Serpent and Siva Worship and Mythology, in Central America, Africa, and Asia and The Origin of Serpent Worship,* Hyde Clarke, M.A.I., and C. Staniland Wake, M.A.I., New York: J. W. Bouton, 1877.

Webster's Seventh New Collegiate Dictionary. Springfield, MA: G. & C. Merriam Company, 1967.

Weiss, Peter. "Matter's Missing Piece Shows Up," *Science News* 158, no. 5 (July 29, 2000), 68.

———. "Seeking the Mother of All Matter." *Science News,* 158, no. 9 (2000).

Wigoder, Geoffrey. *Encyclopedic Dictionary of Judaica.* New York: Leon Amiel Publisher, 1974.

World Book 2002 Standard Edition. Microsoft, 2002.

Wu, C. "Buckyballs Can Come From Outer Space." *Science News,* 157, no. 13 (2000).

INDEX